SHAMELESS AUDACITY

IN THE PITFALLS OF LIFE

THE BOOK OF JOB OFFERS LIGHT
FOR LIFE'S JOURNEY

DR. RUDY MORGAN

Published by Dust Jacket Press
Shameless Audacity in the Pitfalls of Life: The Book of Job Offers Light for Life's Journey /
Rudy Morgan

ISBN: 978-1-947671-61-4

Dust Jacket Press
P.O. Box 721243
Oklahoma City, OK 73172
www.dustjacket.com

dustjacket
www.dustjacket.com

DEDICATION

I begin this dedication by thanking first of all my dear friend Anthony Turrentine, who in 2017 suggested to our Bible study group that we go through the book of Job. Anthony is a positive, contemporary, Job-like friend. This timely suggestion opened a world of personal blessing, and I pray it will also be a tremendous positive motivation to you as you go through this book. I am someone who praises the Lord for every word in the Bible, which gives new enlightenment at every reading.

Second, on a Friday night in August 2018 two of my dear friends in ministry, Mark Lawrence and Victor Price, visited our home in New York City. I thank them both for the hours that these godly servants of Christ struggled through, facing horrendous traffic while traveling from Massachusetts to New York to visit their boyhood friend. Several times during their journey it would have made sense to stop, turn around, and possibly try to visit on another day.

I got the impression after their joyful, prayerful, and encouraging visit that the hours spent with them were God-ordained. I gathered that they arrived back in Massachusetts around 2 am. Mark and Victor had been indeed positive, Job-like friends. Later I began to sense from the conversation with my friends that the months I had spent with our Bible study group reflecting on the heart of Job (which included my dear wife, Ann, another positive, Job-like friend) should be put on paper. In doing so, others would have this opportunity to draw closer to Jesus in their journeys through life.

Third, I dedicate this book to the many who have taken the time to pray for me through the journey of suffering and challenges I have continued to face in the past years. I especially thank my mother, Pearl, who prays for me every single day without fail, and I treasure that. This book is one of victory in Christ, shameless audacity in loving God, hope, and Christian growth and is far more than a Bible study.

It is also dedicated to you who might one day face a tough season or might be going through severe suffering and challenges today. To God goes all the glory for every page in this book.

Job, a servant of God, is a man for all the seasons we face. God bless the broken roads and hours of significant challenges in the lives of all people who read. Remember: His grace and powers are not limited. May many "wailing" days for the reader be channeled to intense worship and encouragement. Out of every pitfall in life, rise well every time through Christ.

"We also glory in our sufferings, because we know that suffering produces perseverance; perseverance, character; and character, hope" (Romans 5:3–4).

CONTENTS

FOREWORD

It was in the year 1969, approximately fifty years ago, that the paths of Rudy Morgan and me intersected. We had both passed the Common Entrance Examinations for the same high school, Wolmer's Boys. Little did we know that our paths would still be so closely linked fifty years later. Now he is Dr. Rev. Rudy Morgan, and here I am in 2019 privileged to be writing a foreword for his book, *Shameless Audacity in the Pitfalls of Life.*

Rudy has been a very close friend over the many years since we first met. He had the privilege of leading me to Christ as a teenager, for which I am forever grateful. This came after he himself had become a Christian after a very tragic occurrence in his life. He became a shamelessly audacious witness for the Lord, a witness that has not diminished to this day. It is no surprise that his book would include the words "shameless audacity" as this speaks to the man who for so many years has boldly proclaimed and lived Christ in this world of ours.

Dr. Morgan and I are both ordained ministers in the Church of the Nazarene since 1984. We both attended Caribbean Nazarene Theological College (CNTC), now Caribbean Nazarene College (CNC), which is located in Trinidad and Tobago. We both served in Jamaica for some years after graduating from CNTC before he and his wife, Ann, left for the United States. This family would eventually include two lovely daughters. During this time Dr. Morgan and Ann, with shameless audacity, started several churches and are currently in the process of starting one more. In the midst of all of this, he has faced and continues to face some health challenges that probably would have shaken the core of most of us. However, today this book rises out of the ashes as a personal testimony and also as a challenge to humankind to follow the Lord and Saviour Jesus Christ and in doing so to be shamelessly audacious in living daily for Him, especially if, like the biblical character Job, you have been experiencing some seriously difficult personal pitfalls.

Shameless Audacity in the Pitfalls of Life is an easy yet enlightening and very effective read. It is a look into the life of Job and how he personally handled his own unsolicited pitfalls. It is also a book about how we should handle our own pitfalls, unsolicited or otherwise. This book is an easy ready also because of its personal nature. The author is not afraid to give us a view into his life and the afflictions he faced and continues to face to this day. Even though this has not been easy for him to do, it connects with readers because of its very personal content. One wants to find out how Job dealt with his issues but also how the author has dealt with the pitfalls he has faced. Dr. Morgan writes with words that are generally easy to follow and not overly academic. The book is also not a long one and so is quite reader-friendly.

Shameless Audacity in the Pitfalls of Life is also quite enlightening. Many have heard about the man Job, the main character of this book, and how wealthy he was, how he had a precious family, and how God "boasted" about how upright he was and how he shunned evil (Job 1:8). Yet God allowed Job to lose almost everything without any explanation. How Job handled these pitfalls is what Dr. Morgan deals with in his book and how we can also handle our pitfalls.

One area of enlightenment for me is when Dr. Morgan talks about the silence of God. This was new for me in reading about Job. He talks about God being able to trust us because we are shamelessly audacious in our love for Him; He is able to trust us with His silence. It is not easy to trust God when He is silent while you are expecting to hear something from Him. Yet God expected Job to keep trusting Him and so He expects it of us as well. This is not the only place of enlightenment as you will find out when you read this book.

Another thing that was enlightening was the fact that I don't remember ever including "Mrs. Job" in the happy ending the story. It was she who had told her husband to curse God and die. Yet she, like her husband, would have been experiencing deep pain with the tremendous loss of family and wealth. We don't read about her death and so it is safe to assume she was there when God turned things around for Job. The author's focus on Job's wife is enlightening and worth the read.

Shameless Audacity in the Pitfalls of Life is also a book the reader will find quite effective in helping us apply the truths of the book of Job. For example, in chapter four Dr. Morgan highlights that Job's friends said some things that were not necessarily wrong but were not true for Job. We all need to be wise in what we say to persons who are going through their pitfalls. Pitfalls are not always a result of sin in the lives of persons as the book of Job so adequately illustrates in Job's case.

Chapter five of Morgan's book illustrates something that is both enlightening and effective. The author speaks to the many questions given to Job by God. God needed to let Job know who was in charge, and He did so with some questions that left no doubt that He was in charge. I had read the book of Job several times, but this had not stood out to me. Yet the author highlights this and in so doing effectively illustrates that even though Job was a man God could boast about, he was only what he was because of God.

Dr. Morgan, thank you for your faithful friendship over the years and taking the time to write this book. Thank you for taking the time to make the book of Job more meaningful to us, your readers. Thank you for sharing those intimate areas of your life. Thank you for a book that is easy to read, enlightening to the heart, and quite effective in teaching truths that should be applied to all our lives. I pray many will read and also become *shamelessly audacious* for our Lord not only when challenged by our personal pitfalls—but always.

Professor Reverend Mark Lawrence
Senior faculty member
Caribbean Nazarene College

ACKNOWLEDGMENTS

The writer is very grateful to all scholars who work meticulously and continuously at accurately transcribing God's revelation in the Holy Bible.

I am grateful for the devotionals written by the late Oswald Chambers. I have enjoyed and benefited from reading these devotionals during years of suffering and challenges. To anyone who has not had exposure to his *My Utmost for His Highest,* you are encouraged to read it online or some other way. Chambers is presently my favorite Christian writer among many I have appreciated over the years. I have included a few of his devotionals as illustrations to enhance the content of this book further.

Rev. Aaron Blache, personal mentor and retired elder in the Church of the Nazarene—thank you for this statement shared with me: "A person may experience suffering or is engaged in an activity to alleviate suffering, but one cannot understand suffering without the benefit of revelation. The book of Job is not just narrative; it is a revelation, and that is why it is so important to study the book of Job."

Thank you to Ann Morgan for taking the time to read and make the necessary grammar corrections. She also suggested convenient ways to better communicate the truths in this book. Praise the Lord for her.

Last, thank you to Jonathan Wright for his meticulous and excellent editing of this project. His thoughtful partnership is greatly appreciated.

INTRODUCTION

This book covering Job examines the theological framework for a useful appreciation of the context and teachings of the Old Testament book called Job. In this book the reader will be able to uncover the personal significance of suffering and painful circumstances as a norm in the human journey. The pages expose readers to a key Bible personality—the patriarch and servant Job. The book of Job is considered to be the first of five books of the Christian Bible in the area devoted to "wisdom poetic literature." Each person reading Job needs to ask God for wisdom to better understand and live the journey exemplified through the life of the servant.

In the following pages we will see Job courageously and confidently staying true to our Lord and God. I have divided the forty-two chapters of Job into six major sections that flow from Job the man lamenting about his life to Job engulfed in the light of God and receiving further grace from God for his spiritual enrichment. We see him growing in his intimacy with God through the pitfalls and challenges that come against him. Persons presently going through diverse types of suffering will benefit and be lifted higher by reading.

It is well to note that all Christians and others who read diligently will be searched to their core by the Holy Spirit as they are exposed to revelations from God through the book of Job. This heart-searching book is written to be a "holy gas station." What I mean is that it should be used as a "fill-up" to continue the journey well in emotionally draining and tricky days.

Each reader should clearly understand that the writer begins with the assumption that the Old Testament book of Job provides nurturing food for healthy spiritual growth and a functional theological paradigm for drawing closer to God. It also challenges us to further shape up to the Spirit-led personal character and follow through with holy behavior in big and small matters.

This book intends to encourage readers to soberly reflect and contemplate personal applications from the journey of Job. There are massive and profound truths of God in this sacred book, and I trust you will frequently meditate on the facts to be exposed.

Upon the reader's completing the book, it is my prayer that he or she will

1. Be challenged and inspired to a more disciplined walk with God—in other words, be more daring and courageous in one's shameless audacity in loving and having total devotion to Jesus Christ.

2. Be encouraged by God's revelation amid suffering and challenges that any reader may be facing. "We

are more than conquerors through him who loved us"
(Romans 8:37).

3. Have enough of a working outline to make better ob-
servations, conversations, and active experimentation
with the Holy Spirit through the revelations in this
book.

4. Consider basic views and theological implications
from Job relating to human suffering, the sovereignty
of God, the role of our familiar enemy the devil, relationships and counsel from brothers and sisters in
Christ, overcoming temptations and tests, intercessory prayer, and persevering in the challenges that
come when walking the Christian faith.

5. Most important of all, be prompted by the Holy
Spirit and see God in a fresh, new way. When we see
God, His miraculous grace keeps flowing abundantly
through us like "rivers of living water" toward other
people. Praise the Lord!

"Share in suffering as a good soldier of Christ Jesus."
(2 Timothy 2:3 CSB)

MY BRIEF STORY OF
SUFFERING AND CHALLENGES

Do I know anything about suffering or going through some hell-like times and challenges in this world? You have your own unique story, but it might be useful to know a little about mine before reading further. "Be very glad—for these trials make you partners with Christ in his suffering" (1 Peter 4:13 NLT). In writing this book I am a fellow sojourner on the road of suffering and heartaches.

In 2010 after fifty years of physical activity and serving people, I faced for the first time a substantial physical obstacle. My days in high school and college included involvement in diverse sports activities. From my early days as a student minister in 1977, I had lived a healthy and active life. There were many days of intense and fruitful Christian ministry in different roles, which included a bivocational ministry for many years.

During several decades of ministry, which included helping birth five new Nazarene churches, like you I had seasons of hard tests and failures, but my Savior, Jesus Christ, showed His favor in beautiful ways. The keeping and sanctifying power of God the Holy Spirit has been real, and I have had so much for which to keep praising and thanking my Lord.

There was a short period in 2001 when I first realized that there are things worse than death in this life. In preparation for a surgical procedure, I had to take a test to see whether or not I had any blockage to my heart. Although it showed that there was nothing wrong, the process triggered a mild stroke. For a few days after this incident I could not remember the content of John 3:16, and the world around me seemed so disorganized for healthy living.

During this time I lost the ability to be focused. The only thing that made any sense for a few days was being able to praise the Lord from the depth of my being and knowing that He was there with me when people on the outside seemed to make no sense. I thought I was going to face the rest of my life with much-dulled memory and comprehension. The Lord physically healed and gave me recovery from that incident. The only lasting trademark from that mild stroke has been the weakening of my hearing over the years.

The obstacle I faced in 2010 started with excruciating pain in my left leg when I attempted to stand or move. I can recall no warning factors preceding my intense pain. Tests eventually showed a synovial cyst between the third and fourth lumbar in my spine. Any movement caused the squeezing of the cyst, and the pain was almost unbearable.

The doctors felt that the best way to deal with this cyst was to remove it. While doing that procedure, they would put in hardware that was intended to strengthen my spine as I grew older and needed added stability. That was the plan. I still recall that my first back surgery was the day before

Thanksgiving 2010 and I expected that I would be fine and should be healing well by Christmas. Everything went well in the operation, and I progressed through the healing process. By January 2011, however, I began realizing that something was wrong because the pain in my back was just as severe as the excruciating pain I had felt in my leg some months before.

A new MRI discovered that a screw from the hardware installed was broken and was touching nerves, and this was now causing the unbelievable pain I felt each day. This was quite unusual, according to the surgeon who had done hundreds of these procedures. The surgeon also suggested that the breaking of these screws was supposed to be in the order of one in a thousand.

The decision that ensued was to have a second surgery and install more substantial hardware that was supposed to be better for me. This surgery occurred near Easter 2011. Again the operation seemed to have been successful, and afterward recovery appeared to be going well with complete healing expected within a few months. However, before the end of the year I felt the same pain again, and it was time to check back in for another MRI.

You might have guessed it—another screw had broken. What an extraordinary coincidence! The only way to properly cure this excruciating pain was to undergo a third surgery. That operation I did not want to do. I had been through enough hardships in my hospital sojourns. So for a couple of years I moved each day with pain, the full extent of which not even my own family understood.

It was not until 2014 when attempting to do active chaplaincy service in hospital visitation that I was forced to admit that this sort of living was more than I could bear, and it was time for another surgery. I proceeded with it, but it was interrupted by complications, and resetting was needed.

In the same area of my lower back a third surgery was completed. Everything seemed to go well, and it was now time to recuperate.

After about a week I was sent home from the hospital. Within twenty-four hours I was back in the hospital because my temperature had reached roughly 106 degrees. I discovered that my body had contamination due to an infection from the previous surgery—and I almost died. An immediate fourth surgery on the lower back was needed to cleanse me from whatever had caused the contamination. This procedure was completed, and I was in the hospital for another period. I was sent home to months of intravenous treatment, during which my loving wife proved to be a gracious and blessed nurse. After these months of touch and go it was now time to return to my day-to-day activity in ministry and work.

After a few months of starting life again, I began feeling pain in my lower back again. It was time for yet another MRI. This time the results showed that the hardware in my back was still in place. However, I was now affected by scoliosis (this had never been a concern before), and one of the suggestions was a fifth surgery that would demand more extensive work near my spine.

Another operation is not something I have wanted to do—and as such, I still live in pain in my lower back to this day. God has not healed me yet and may never do so (it is all in His will as prayer goes up), and after eight years an initial synovial cyst allows me to walk with a cane only for short distances and to stand alone for only a few minutes. Often the only time I feel no pain in my lower back is when I am sitting or lying down.

By now maybe some of you might be feeling sorry for me. Please do not. Seeing Jesus and fellowshipping with my Master in the midst of the unexplained must often be, I suppose, as sweet as what Shadrach, Meshach, and Abednego felt when they saw the Son of Man in the burning fire (Daniel 3) and rejoiced with a "hallelujah time." I am saying that God has been good to me, and I testify to my shameless audacity in loving God amid my pitfalls and the challenges of life.

Since 2017 my kidneys have begun failing. My renal failure has recently reached the place where I was forced to start emergency dialysis in July 2018, and now I go three times each week, and the days ahead are uncertain. We are praying especially for the Lord to allow for the possibility of a kidney transplant. In spite of this, these are some of the best days I have had spiritually because my "spiritual eyes" are firmly fixed on Jesus Christ. The sanctifying power of God is not just something doctrinal for me. There is nothing more important than being wholly surrendered and committed to our Lord even when the world around is unfriendly and sometimes so confusing. I believe I understand a little about living daily under external pressure.

Sometimes God allows things to happen for which there are no explanations shared. We must never forget that spiritual conversations are happening beyond our hearing in the realm of "rulers, against the authorities, . . . the powers of this dark world and . . . the spiritual forces of evil in the heavenly realms" (Ephesians 6:12).

One of my joys now is having opportunities to minister and live joyfully for Christ at the dialysis center in Queens Village, New York.

As I spent a lot of personal time with the book of Job, it did not take long to realize that a lot of what I read had particular significance to me. The joy—not the happiness—of the Lord is my strength. Oswald Chambers puts it better than I can:

> *"These things I have spoken to you, that my joy may remain in you, and that your joy may be full."* —John 15:11. *What was the joy that Jesus had? Joy should not be confused with happiness. It is an insult to Jesus Christ to use the word* happiness *in connection with Him. The joy of Jesus was*

His absolute self-surrender and self-sacrifice to His Father— the joy of doing that which the Father sent Him to do— "who for the joy that was set before He endured the cross . . ." (Hebrews 12:2). *"I delight to do Your will, O my God . . ."* (Psalm 40:8). *Jesus prayed that our joy might continue fulfilling itself until it becomes the same joy as His. Have I allowed Jesus Christ to introduce His joy to me? Living a full and overflowing life does not rest in bodily health, neither in the circumstances, nor even in seeing God's work succeed, but in the perfect understanding of God, and in the same fellowship and oneness with Him that Jesus Himself enjoyed. But the first thing that will hinder this joy is the subtle irritability caused by giving too much thought to our circumstances. Jesus said, "The cares of this world . . . choke the word, and it becomes unfruitful"* (Mark 4:19). (*My Utmost for His Highest,* August 31 devotional)

Remember the stunning instructions of James 1:2–6:

Consider it pure joy, my brothers and sisters, whenever you face trials of many kinds, because you know that the testing of your faith produces perseverance. Let perseverance finish its work so that you may be mature and complete, not lacking anything. If any of you lacks wisdom, you should ask God, who gives generously to all without finding fault, and it will be given to you. But when you ask, you must believe and not doubt, because the one who doubts is like a wave of the sea, blown and tossed by the wind.

The lyrics of "My Tribute" (or "To God be the Glory"), written by André Crouch (who was called by Dr. Billy Graham "the greatest hymn-writer of our age" and "the John Wesley of our age") speak volumes to my soul about unyielding spiritual fortitude.

THOUGHT PATTERS FOR THE BOOK OF JOB—OUTLINES

An easy outline I recommend to the readers for the book of Job is the following:

1. The setting and backdrop for the book of Job (1:1–2:13)
2. The sadness of Job (3:1–26)
3. The speeches and conversations between Job and three friends (4:1–31:40)
   A. Back and forth—how is God related to Job's sin and suffering? (4:1–14:22)
   B. Back and forth—do wicked people always suffer? (15:1–21:34)
   C. Back and forth—is Job guilty of secret sins? (22:1–31:40)
4. The solid negative comments by the younger man Elihu to Job (32:1–37:24)
5. God speaks to Job (38:1–41:34)
6. The secrets to understanding the book of Job
   A. Our eyes opened, for whosoever will (42:1–6
   B. Great ending of divine blessing (42:7–17)

There are many detailed outlines you can find in commentaries, or you can go online and choose one that satisfies the study level at which you want to be involved. In my notes I have paraphrased a longer outline that may be useful to some readers.

1. Prologue (chapters 1–2)
   A. Job's joy (1:1–5)
   B. Job's testings (1:6–2:13)
      i. Satan's first accusations (1:6–12)
      ii. Job's faith despite the loss of family and things (1:13–22)
      iii. Satan's second accusations (2:1–6)
      iv. Job's faith during personal suffering (2:7–10)
      v. The introduction to three prestigious friends of Job (2:11–13)

2. Job's opening lament (chapter 3)

3. The first cycle of conversations and speeches (chapters 4–14)
   A. Eliphaz (chapters 4–5)
   B. Job's reply (chapters 6–7)
   C. Bildad (chapter 8)
   D. Job's response (chapters 9–10)
   E. Zophar (chapter 11)
   F. Job's answer (chapters 12–14)

One key verse [Key verses] for many of us to emulate is from the lips of Job: "But he knows the way that I take; when he has tested me, I will come forth as gold. My feet have closely followed his steps; I have kept to his way without turning aside" (Job 23:10–11). Do likewise in your life!

After finishing this book, there are excellent Bible commentators to improve your time with the publication of Job further, but one I recommend is the renowned commentator Adam Clarke. He states that the purpose of the book of Job is "to justify the wisdom and goodness of God in matters of human suffering and especially to show that all suffering is not punitive."

Be willing always to give God "elbow room" to show you the Scriptures at a broader and more productive level.

1

The Laments of Job
(Chapter 3)

F or some readers the recorded laments of Job may seem a strange place to begin our conversations with the book of Job. However, most people will appreciate the human emotion of being overwhelmed by circumstances and being at the place where all doors of hope are far away when the fibers of one's heart wish that everything would come to an end. Guess what—Job had those feelings too. Thus he asks, "Why didn't I die at birth, my first breath out of the womb my last?" (3:11 MSG). The same man noted in folk- lore for his patience also had seasons that asked, "What is the purpose of my existence?" As such, I believe the better place in our modern world to understand and evaluate Job begins best in chapter three.

The word got around that a well-known community leader and a friend of God was going through tremendous suffering.

> *When Job's three friends, Eliphaz the Teman- ite, Bildad the Shuhite and Zophar the Naama- thite, heard about all the troubles that had come*

upon him, they set out from their homes and met together by agreement to go and sympathize with him and comfort him. When they saw him from a distance, they could hardly recognize him; they began to weep aloud, and they tore their robes and sprinkled dust on their heads. Then they sat on the ground with him for seven days and seven nights. No one said a word to him, because they saw how great his suffering was. (2:11–13)

It was very commendable for the friends of Job to hang around this man for extended periods, who not only looked very terrible but also, I suspect, had a bad odor and would have needed all sorts of body cleansing. Job speaking of himself says,

> *"He [God] has alienated my family from me;*
> *my acquaintances are completely estranged*
> *from me.*
> *My relatives have gone away;*
> *my closest friends have forgotten me.*
> *My guests and my female servants count me*
> *a foreigner;*
> *they look on me as on a stranger.*
> *I summon my servant, but he does not answer,*
> *though I beg him with my own mouth.*
> *My breath is offensive to my wife;*

I am loathsome to my own family.
Even the little boys scorn me;
  when I appear, they ridicule me.
All my intimate friends detest me;
  those I love have turned against me.
I am nothing but skin and bones;
  I have escaped only by the skin of my teeth."
(19:13–20)

In my notes over the years I find an anonymous quote that reads, "Sufferers cannot extricate themselves from the hole called grief. They need a rope. Sufferers need someone at the other end to 'pull.'" I need help in my journey of suffering and challenges, and so do you.

The person unsaved from sin, or who is outside of a relationship with Christ, is very limited in trying to address how to know what is accurate and helpful in dire predicaments, mostly because he or she does not benefit from openness to God's revelations in the Holy Bible. Many readers may need comfort and guidance. Other people may be wondering where God is on the journey of "second chances," which He has offered to some of you.

In one of our Wednesday night Bible study gatherings my "Job-like friend" Anthony shared with our group the following experience in which he needed to ask himself, "What now?" God has given him another chance in life. The following was his story.

A bump woke him up. He lifted his head, and his arms folded on the steering wheel of his vehicle where he had fallen asleep. There was pitch blackness surrounding Anthony, and he noticed that his foot had been on the accelerator going seventy miles per hour. As he veered off the road, a telephone pole was approaching his van. His only reaction was to turn the wheel to the left to keep from hitting the pole straight on. Still there was a big bang, and time seemed to freeze for a moment. He found himself dragged under the fifteen-passenger van, and his body absorbed much of the pavement of the road.

"What now?" he wondered. He started talking to God, asking if this was the way he was going to die. Then all at once the van came to a complete stop! At that moment he realized that he was still alive. The vehicle had hit the telephone pole and had been thrown across the street and slammed into a shack. Immediately Anthony rolled out from under his van, and people from nearby ran to his aid.

The van was destroyed, but by the grace of God his life had been spared, and Anthony received a second chance. God had rescued him from death, and now the question was what he would do with this great privilege. He shared that he now lives an active life for his Lord and Savior, determined to

love and serve his Lord with all his heart, mind,
and soul. He now experiences a heightened fervor to
tell anyone, focusing on Jesus and Him alone.

Seeing God through the journey of Job provides the privilege to taste and rejoice in how sweet Jesus is in an intimate relationship with Him. Praise the Lord!

The servant of the Lord is quoted as saying,

"May the day of my birth perish,
and the night that said, 'A boy is conceived!'
That day—may it turn to darkness;
may God above not care about it;
may no light shine on it.
May gloom and utter darkness claim it once more;
may a cloud settle over it;
may blackness overwhelm it.
That night—may thick darkness seize it;
may it not be included among the days of the year
nor be entered in any of the months." (3:3–6)

What should be the overarching guidelines for truth for God's children? Is it "what I know to be truth revealed from God's Word" or "how I feel" that should be my guide in my worst and challenging days? Most readers, I suspect, will acknowledge that the truths and reports of God's Word are the bottom lines for living the Christian life as being most important. We will find that this was also true for the patriarch Job as his life unfolded before us in the Holy Writ.

We are not "bad Christians" when going through substantial pitfalls or suffering in life and wishing we had never been born. Brazen honesty with our emotions and selves can often be an essential unlocking key to honest conversations and intimacy with our Lord. God understands the unbearable.

Physical pain is very debilitating and is enough on its own to destroy confidence and self-worth. However, my sadness over the past years goes beyond physical illnesses. For example, some scars change a person's life forever. On March 19, 1971, at the impressionable age of thirteen, I was at home in Spanish Town, Jamaica. I was the last one to see and hear his voice as blood gushed from my father's (John's) body from a grave knife-inflicted wound to his neck. I still feel emotional pain as I write this book many years later. As I look back, I could have quickly died also.

I admire the three friends of Job (Eliphaz, Bildad, and Zophar) who initially seemed interested in being there for Job in his season of sorrow. They seemed to care, and when this is done well in the New Testament body of Christ, so much good is accomplished and burdens are made lighter and bearable for the man or woman who is going through difficulties.

A warm church body can give the wounded believer a sense of stability made possible by Jesus, through His great act of love and grace demonstrated in the cross. However, we will later find out that the friends of Job came to converse with Job with underlining agendas that were distorted by cultural beliefs and not necessarily openness to honest conversation. Giving ungodly counsel can also destroy true fellowship in today's church anywhere in the world.

Unfortunately, this is still happening in Christ's church today. Sometimes very unwise advice can come from "wise" people. It is so vital for our daily intimacy with the Holy Spirit to be the number-one detail in our lives even when we have the privilege of enjoying some good Christian friends. Intimacy with God must override even our love for our closest family members and friends.

I am one of those who believes that there was a real, historical Job who lived over 1,500 years before the coming of Christ. Job is not merely a literary character made up and designed to teach living lessons to the human family. He lived, and the Holy Spirit used him to guide our daily experiences as long as the human family exists.

Many Bible teachers believe that the book of Job was the first chronological Bible book inspired by the Holy Spirit. I am from that theological trend of thinking. Why would Job be the first book written of the sixty-six books in the Bible? Remember: the most common symptom and ramification of human evil is the pain or suffering that all human beings face in one form or another because of our great fall into sin in the Garden of Eden. Sin and its horrible ramifications are an original part of the character damaged among the human family. Romans 5:12 says, "Sin entered the world through one man, and death through sin, and in this way death came to all people, because all sinned."

No wonder the light from Job shining for the sad human family would be a paramount message that God would want to share loudly and apparently to all generations who face the consequences of suffering in one form or another.

I remember discussing with a group in a hospital the situation of an elderly woman whose husband had passed away a few years before. She now lives alone. This lady had four children and several grandchildren but did not seem to have close relationships with them, and she felt alone. The faith of this older lady was weak, and she struggled with whether God heard her prayers. Tens of thousands of other persons can multiply this kind of story.

Maybe the reader relates more closely to a young adult with a Jamaican ethnic background whom I spent time with while she struggled with a substantial drug problem. This lady had a religious history from a young age. Was there any hope for her, having suffered so much already from the choices she had made? Some readers may be asking themselves if there is any hope for them in the particular situations they face today.

The two people mentioned previously had stories different from Job's as they relate to suffering, but God does not ignore the cry of anyone who suffers, and that includes you. You may never have felt that you are saintly like Job, but at some point you have made similar statements like those of Job.

Most will agree that Job 1 and 2 and parts of 42 are prose. The rest of Job is poetry, but all of Job is God's revelation founded in historical facts. In the book of Job you will not always find common sense easy to understand, but you will see "revelation sense" challenging readers to stand firm in faith for Christ and a lot of God sense. Everything recorded in Job is real, even the cynical and human emotional statements from the main character who speaks to the trauma expressed in his feelings:

> *"Why did I not perish at birth,*
> *and die as I came from the womb?*
> *Why were there knees to receive me*
> *and breasts that I might be nursed?*
> *For now, I would be lying down in peace;*
> *I would be asleep and at rest*
> *with kings and rulers of the earth,*
> *who built for themselves places now lying in*
> *ruins, with princes who had gold,*
> *who filled their houses with silver.*
>
> *Or why was I not hidden away in the ground like*
> *a stillborn child,*

like an infant who never saw the light of day?
There the wicked cease from turmoil,
  and there the weary are at rest.

 Captives also enjoy their ease;
  they no longer hear the slave driver's shout.
The small and the great are there,
  and the slaves are freed from their owners.

Why is light given to those in misery,
  and life to the bitter of soul,
to those who long for death that does not come,
  who search for it more than for hidden treasure,
who are filled with gladness
  and rejoice when they reach the grave?
Why is life given to a man
  whose way is hidden,
  whom God has hedged in?
For sighing has become my daily food;
  my groans pour out like water.
What I feared has come upon me;
  what I dreaded has happened to me.
I have no peace, no quietness;
  I have no rest, but only turmoil."
(3:11–26)

Do you recall the events on Mount Carmel in which God received great glory through the prophet Elijah standing up victoriously against the hoards of Baal's prophets (1 Kings 18)?

This drama was followed by King Ahab and Jezebel going in search of and seeking the destruction of the prophet Elijah. The human servant reached a place at which the Bible said,

> *Elijah was afraid and ran for his life. When he came to Beersheba in Judah, he left his servant there, while he went a day's journey into the wilderness. He came to a broom bush, sat down under it and prayed that he might die. "I have had enough, Lord," he said. "Take my life; I am no better than my ancestors." Then he lay down under the bush and fell asleep.* (1 Kings 19:3–5)

Have you been there yourself? I know the meaning of "down in the valleys."

A searching heart and a notable anonymous writer of a poem titled "Listen" says well what a lot of hurting people ask or want us to hear:

> *When I ask you to listen to me,*
> *And you start giving advice,*
> *You have not done what I asked.*
> *When I ask you to listen to me,*
> *And you begin to tell me why I shouldn't*
>   *feel that way,*
> *You are trampling my feelings.*

When I asked you to listen to me,
And you feel you have to do something to
solve my problem,
You have failed me, strange as that may seem.
Listen! All I asked was that you listen,
not talk or do—hear me.
Advice is cheap: fifty cents will get you
both Dear Abby and Abigail Van Buren
in the same newspaper!
And I can do for myself: I am not helpless.
Maybe discouraged and faltering,
but not helpless.

When you do something for me that I can
and need to do myself,
You contribute to my fear and weakness.
But when you accept as a simple fact that
I do not feel what I feel, no matter how
irrational,
Then I quit trying to convince you and get
about the business of understanding what
is behind this irrational feel,
And that is clear, the answers are obvious,
and I don't need advice.
Irrational feelings make sense when we
understand what's behind them.

Perhaps that's why prayer sometimes works
for some people.
God is mute and doesn't give advice or
try to fix things;
Just listen and let you work it out yourself.
[As the writer of this book I challenge the
theology in the previous stanza in this
poem, but not the sincere honesty
expressed]

So, please listen and just hear me.
And if you want to talk, wait a minute
for your turn; and I will listen to you.

The apostle James and a writer I am thrilled by puts it far
better than I can in describing what God-like living looks like
and how it is best lived:

My dear brothers and sisters, take note of
this: Everyone should be quick to listen, slow to
speak and slow to become angry, because human
anger does not produce the righteousness that God
desires. Therefore, get rid of all moral filth and the
evil that is so prevalent and humbly accept the
word planted in you, which can save you. Do not
merely listen to the word, and so deceive yourselves.
Do what it says. Anyone who listens to the word

but does not do what it says is like someone who looks at his face in a mirror and, after looking at himself, goes away and immediately forgets what he looks like. But whoever looks intently into the perfect law that gives freedom, and continues in it-not forgetting what they have heard, but doing it—they will be blessed in what they do. Those who consider themselves religious and yet do not keep a tight rein on their tongues deceive themselves, and their religion is worthless. (James 1:19–26)

Job 3 is full of lamentations (like funeral songs), but there are many other places in this book that Job speaks similarly like the prophet Jeremiah as he grieved about the destruction of Jerusalem in the Old Testament book of Lamentations. As a positive reminder in chapter 5 of the same book, there is also an encouraging prayer for God's mercy. Lamenting by anyone does not mean that the doors of hope are no more. We will find that out of the lamenting experiences of Job, he was able to draw closer to God.

Pain and suffering in life are things we all can identify with and must face in one form or another. That is probably why many around the world identify so well with songwriter and singer Bob Marley as he quotes lines from Psalm 137. Some may even think Marley wrote the lines "By the rivers of Babylon," but he did not. Job, if he could have read the psalm, might have equated its sentiments with how he felt in the third chapter of Job. Psalm 137 reads,

By the rivers of Babylon, we sat and wept
when we remembered Zion.
There on the poplars
we hung our harps,
for there our captors asked us for songs,
our tormentors demanded songs of joy;
they said, "Sing us one of the songs of Zion!"

How can we sing the songs of the Lord
while in a foreign land?
If I forget you, Jerusalem,
may my right hand forget its skill.
May my tongue cling to the roof of my mouth
if I do not remember you,
if I do not consider Jerusalem
my highest joy.

Remember, Lord, what the Edomites did
on the day Jerusalem fell.
"Tear it down," they cried,
"tear it down to its foundations!"
Daughter Babylon, doomed to destruction,
happy is the one who repays you
according to what you have done to us.
Happy is the one who seizes your infants
and dashes them against the rocks.
(Psalm 137:1–9)

The servant Job in his anguish and the present ruin that has overcome his life puts his feelings this way in 3:24–26: "Instead of bread I get groans for my supper, then leave the table and vomit my anguish. The worst of my fears has come true, what I've dreaded most has happened. My response is shattered; my peace destroyed. No rest for me, ever—death has invaded life" (MSG). He feels like this, but there is a back story that Job knows nothing.

What has God been doing and allowing in the life of Job? What is God doing and allowing in all of our lives that we know nothing about and may never know on this side of eternity? To better understand the surrounding circumstances, it is now necessary to examine Job 1–2.

When I feel anything the way Job felt, a 1976 song written by John Stallings called "Learning to Lean" gives comfort to my spiritual journey. Learn it if you have not already.

My mother named me after Rudyard Kipling, who was an English poet who lived from 1865 to 1936. The poem most remembered among his many writings was one titled "If." I believe the patriarch Job would have liked to reflect on the following words. I think you should too in seeking a stable focus in whatever circumstances you are facing today.

> *If you can keep your head when all about you*
> *Are losing theirs and blaming it on you;*
> *If you can trust yourself when all men doubt you,*
> *But make allowance for their doubting too:*

If you can wait and not be tired by waiting,
  Or, being lied about, don't deal in lies,
Or being hated don't give way to hating,
  And yet don't look too good, nor talk too wise;

If you can dream—and not make dreams
  your master;
  If you can think—and not make thoughts
  your aim,
If you can meet with Triumph and Disaster
  And treat those two impostors just the same;
If you can bear to hear the truth you've spoken
  Twisted by knaves to make a trap for fools,
Or watch the things you gave your life to, broken,
  And stoop and build'em up with worn-out tools;

If you can make one heap of all your winnings
  And risk it on one turn of pitch-and-toss,
And lose, and start again at your beginnings,
  And never breathe a word about your loss;
If you can force your heart and nerve and sinew
  To serve your turn long after they are gone,
And so hold on when there is nothing in you
  Except for the Will which says to them:
  "Hold on";

If you can talk with crowds and keep your virtue,
Or walk with kings—nor lose the common
touch,
If neither foes nor loving friends can hurt you,
If all men count with you, but none too much:
If you can fill the unforgiving minute
With sixty seconds' worth of distance run,
Yours is the Earth and everything that's in it,
And—which is more—you'll be a Man, my son!

2

The Literal Background that Surrounded Job
(Chapters 1–2)

Where does Job begin chronologically in the Holy Writ, and what are those essential truths that we need to absorb thoroughly? The righteous living of God's children is something God loves and adores intently. For Satan to get between God and His children, he must get us to be comfortable in sinful thoughts, attitudes, and living.

We see in the book of Job that the principles of suffering and challenges for God's people have in their background a titanic struggle between Satan and God. In this chapter you will also discover the genesis for the impact enunciated in the title of this book: *Shameless Audacity in the Pitfalls of Life*.

Someone not known was used by the Holy Spirit to write the story of Job. This writer reminds every disciple of Christ who suffers (and any other person who will listen) that above every other wisdom learned in this life should be loving God more than the gifts He gives. Trust the wise goodness of God even when circumstances and challenges blind us. Have I placed my confidence in God alone, not in His blessings or material abundance? Do I grasp it deep down?

"I am God Almighty"—El-Shaddai, the All-Powerful God (Genesis 17:1).

So much of our journey through life is beyond the power of human wisdom to fathom, and that is how Job begins in the first two chapters. We see a very realistic, compelling drama that wrestles with the knowledge, justice, and love of the Almighty God.

"Righteous sufferers [and each person has a choice] must trust in, acknowledge, serve and submit to the omniscient and omnipotent Sovereign, realizing that some suffering is the result of unseen, spiritual conflicts between the kingdom of God and kingdom of Satan—between the kingdom of light and the kingdom of darkness (reflect on Ephesians 6: 10–18)" (https://www.biblestudytools.com/job/).

In the first conversation in this book between God and Satan, we see recorded the following interaction (Job was never told any of the text as far as we know):

> *Then the Lord said to Satan, "Have you consid-*
> *ered my servant Job? There is no one on earth like*
> *him; he is blameless and upright, a man who fears*
> *God and shuns evil."*

> *"Does Job fear God for nothing?" Satan re-*
> *plied. "Have you not put a hedge around him and*
> *his household and everything he has? You have*
> *blessed the work of his hands so that his flocks and*
> *herds are spread throughout the land. But now*

stretch out your hand and strike everything he has, and he will surely curse you to your face."

The Lord said to Satan, "Very well, then, everything he has is in your power, but on the man himself do not lay a finger."

Then Satan went out from the presence of the Lord.

One day when Job's sons and daughters were feasting and drinking wine at the oldest brother's house, a messenger came to Job and said, "The oxen were plowing and the donkeys were grazing nearby, and the Sabeans attacked and made off with them. They put the servants to the sword, and I am the only one who has escaped to tell you!"

While he was still speaking, another messenger came and said, "The fire of God fell from the heavens and burned up the sheep and the servants, and I am the only one who has escaped to tell you!"

While he was still speaking, another messenger came and said, "The Chaldeans formed three raiding parties and swept down on your camels and made off with them. They put the servants to the sword, and I am the only one who has escaped to tell you!"

While he was still speaking, yet another messenger came and said, "Your sons and daughters were feasting and drinking wine at the oldest brother's house, when suddenly a mighty wind swept in from the desert and struck the four corners of the house. It collapsed on them and they are dead, and I am the only one who has escaped to tell you!"

At this, Job got up and tore his robe and shaved his head. Then he fell to the ground in worship and said:

"Naked I came from my mother's womb, and naked I will depart.

The Lord gave and the Lord has taken away; may the name of the Lord be praised."

In all this, Job did not sin by charging God with wrongdoing. (1:8–22)

A wealthy man from an ethical and well-known family lived in Uz (1:1–3). Some scholars have strong inclinations as to where this country was. I am one of those preferring to say that I do not know for sure where Uz was. The most important facet about the description of Job's lifestyle was that he was "blameless and upright; he feared God and shunned evil" (1:1). In talking about the size of his family and animals, the number seven is mentioned more than once. Throughout the Scriptures this number repeatedly symbolizes God's overview of perfection and what is beautiful in His eyes.

There is nothing wrong or unholy in receiving and enjoying great material blessings from God. Why doesn't God give everybody plenty of material blessings? I don't know—He does not share the reasoning used as to how He decides which people (both righteous and sinful people) receive more material blessings in this world.

However, what I am sure of is the following: "Don't be deceived, my dear brothers and sisters. Every good and perfect gift is from above, coming down from the Father of the heavenly lights, who does not change like shifting shadows" (James 1:16–17).

In Job 1:5 we read, "When a period of feasting had run its course, Job would make arrangements for them to be purified. Early in the morning he would sacrifice a burnt offering for each of them, thinking, 'Perhaps my children have sinned and cursed God in their hearts.' This was Job's regular custom." Job diligently served as the priest in his own home and clan. What an excellent, positive example of pure goodness and discipline!

At the end of the book of Job (chapter 42) he is still serving as a priest or as God's intercessor and go-between for neighbors and friends. In our most excellent days or seasons of pain and suffering in this life, do not lose the importance of being a vessel out of which the Holy Spirit flows rivers of living water toward others (John 7:38).

Lydia Baxter wrote the words and William H. Doane applied the music to the hymn "Take the Name of Jesus." Be like Job and take the name of Jesus wherever and whenever you go anywhere. This great hymn says,

Take the name of Jesus with you,
　　Child of sorrow and of woe.
It will joy and comfort give you;
　　Take it, then, where'er you go.

Precious name, O how sweet!
　　Hope of earth and joy of heav'n!
Precious name, O how sweet!
　　Hope of earth and joy of heav'n!

Take the name of Jesus ever,
　　As a shield from every snare.
If temptations round you gather,
　　Breathe that holy name in prayer.

O the precious name of Jesus!
　　How it thrills our souls with joy,
When His loving arms receive us,
　　And His songs our tongues employ!

At the name of Jesus bowing,
　　Falling prostrate at His feet,

King of Kings in heav'n we'll crown Him
When our journey is complete.

Initially Satan took material things away from Job. In a follow-up conversation Satan was allowed to touch the body of Job profoundly without taking his life. Job walked with God in every circumstance.

> *Job is famous for a life of such "troubling" moments. Indeed, his losses were deep and many. Just moments after losing all his livestock, he learns of the simultaneous death of all his ten children. Job's profound grief evidenced in his response: he "tore his robe and shaved his head" (1:20). His words in that painful hour make me think Job knew the practice of gratitude, for he acknowledges that God had given him everything he had lost (v.21). How else could he worship during such incapacitating grief? The practice of daily gratitude can't erase the magnitude of pain we feel in seasons of loss. Job questioned and grappled through his grief as the rest of the book describes.* (From the devotional by Kirsten Holmberg for December 23, 2018, *Our Daily Bread*.)

In my physical body there is so much weakness, but in Christ I have Jesus's resurrected life to take with me wherever

I go, and I do not lose heart. I rejoice and encourage my soul reflecting on the words of the apostle Paul: "Therefore we do not lose heart. Though outwardly we are wasting away, yet inwardly we are renewed day by day. For our light and momentary troubles are achieving for us an eternal glory that far outweighs them all. So we fix our eyes not on what is seen, but on what is unseen, since what is seen is temporary, but what is unseen is eternal" (2 Corinthians 4:16–18).

I believe the apostle Peter would have been familiar with the stories surrounding the servant Job, and maybe he thought of him as he encouraged the early Christian church and all of us while going through hell, suffering, testings, and tribulations. "Be alert and of sober mind. Your enemy the devil prowls around like a roaring lion looking for someone to devour. Resist him, standing firm in the faith, because you know that the family of believers throughout the world is undergoing the same kind of sufferings" (1 Peter 5:8–9).

Satan seeks the destruction of every human being, especially those who choose to walk the way of the cross. During the period that Job suffered, the main human characters did not know the spiritual conversations taking place in spiritual realms. God was not allowing the approaches of Satan in heavenly realms for haphazard reasons, and He was not allowing the pains of Job for no reason. So on another day in chapter two, Satan approaches God again. Nothing happens to God's children without the knowledge and will of God. The Scriptures say,

On another day the angels came to present themselves before the Lord, and Satan also came with them to present himself before him. And the Lord said to Satan, "Where have you come from?"

Satan answered the Lord, "From roaming throughout the earth, going back and forth on it."

Then the Lord said to Satan, "Have you considered my servant Job? There is no one on earth like him; he is blameless and upright, a man who fears God and shuns evil. And he still maintains his integrity, though you incited me against him to ruin him without any reason."

"Skin for skin!" Satan replied. "A man will give all he has for his own life. But now stretch out your hand and strike his flesh and bones, and he will surely curse you to your face."

The Lord said to Satan, "Very well, then, he is in your hands; but you must spare his life."

So Satan went out from the presence of the Lord and afflicted Job with painful sores from the soles of his feet to the crown of his head. Then Job took a piece of broken pottery and scraped himself with it as he sat among the ashes.

His wife said to him, "Are you still maintaining your integrity? Curse God and die!"

> *He replied, "You are talking like a fool-*
> *ish woman. Shall we accept good from God, and*
> *not trouble?"*
>
> *In all this, Job did not sin in what he said.*
> (2:1–10)

Please reflect when considering the words spoken by "Mrs. Job" in 2:9. I have heard negative comments about this lady. Remember: the wife of Job is speaking from the standpoint of anger and unbelievable pain. She has lost all of her children and now sees her husband as a shell of a man, probably even hard to physically recognize. You and I do not understand what she was facing. I wonder if Mr. and Mrs. Job had any intelligent and lengthy conversations during this period of great physical suffering.

One of the most foolish things I hear from well-meaning people to other people suffering is "I understand how you feel." We do not understand, and you are encouraged to run from comments like these in the hours of struggle by other people. I also hear people say to others going through "hell," "Keep your focus and don't be confused," or "These things happen for a reason if you love the Lord." Those are the wrong perspectives to share as a counselor and for someone who loves the Lord very much. Most people are not strong enough to deal with big pitfalls and unfortunate circumstances.

Mayo Angelo once said what was so right for Job's life,

You may shoot me with your words,
You may cut me with your eyes,
You may kill me with your hatefulness,
But still, like air, I'll rise.

A good friend will look for physical, cognitive, emotional, or behavioral reactions in a hurting person that may require continuing individual support. Be a good friend. Mother Theresa once said, "Kind words can be short and easy to speak, but their echoes are truly endless."

As an example, Jesus shared a parable in Luke 11:5–8 that took me a long while to grasp. Sometimes the friendship of our Lord is shrouded. In the parable Jesus says,

"Suppose you have a friend, and you go to him at midnight and say, 'Friend, lend me three loaves of bread; a friend of mine on a journey has come to me, and I have no food to offer him.' And suppose the one inside answers, 'Don't bother me. The door is already locked, and my children and I are in bed. I can't get up and give you anything.' I tell you, even though he will not get up and give you the bread because of friendship, yet because of your shameless audacity he will surely get up and give you as much as you need."

In this story told by Jesus, it appears that the man did not care for his friend. And that is how our loving heavenly

Father will sometimes seem to His children as it did to Job in his human travail. I believe Job felt this way a lot throughout his journey of great need and suffering. Remember that Jesus is not an unkind friend. The time will come when everything will have an explanation because of your own "shameless audacity" exhibited in your Christian faith. It will take the grace of God, courage, bravery, and holiness. Job was tested for all he was worth, and so will all of Jesus's disciples. God will give you enough "Christian swagger" to complement your walk of faith in God's light.

To the many who have been hurt and ignored in diverse ways by others, be willing to go the extra mile (Matthew 5:38–44) because of the love of Christ and the solid strength He will give to you. I am not asking you to pretend that the adverse circumstances you face are not real, but do what is not your duty or easy to do and choose to will and do what shameless audacity gives and empowers as holy directions in the Bible. This living will continue to receive the mighty favor of God in your life.

In this book I am challenging readers to shameless audacity in loving and trusting Jesus in your faith journey. Stop and focus on being hugely fearless in your boldness, your belief, and your confidence in Jesus even when He seems silent in the pain you face. I am daring readers (especially those living through pain presently as servants of Christ) to take the "risky journey" filled with shameless audacity in their faith walk. It will be the most rewarding adventure you could ever experience as a disciple of God—as Job experienced.

Job tells his wife to accept both pleasant and trouble from God, but in going through hell, Job did not sin. Hallelujah! One of the many unanswered questions I have about the book of Job is whether the same "Mrs. Job" in chapters one and two, who lost all her children, material possessions, and almost her husband, is the same Job's wife in chapter forty-two given the privilege of mothering ten more children in that last period of the patriarch's life. When one is going through great sadness and says awful things, don't give up on the person.

The following are comments for readers to consider in thinking about the blindness that surrounded the main character before moving on with the Bible story. "The Lord said to Satan, 'Very well, then, he is in your hands; but you must spare his life.'" Satan dared not disobey the command of our Lord. Our Lord is King of Kings and Lord of Lords, and He is always sovereign and is still in control. Nothing dilutes the absolute authority of God. We are also referring to all stories of life dealing with suffering, challenges, and tragedies. Even one's ability to use the bathroom can occur only because of God's permission.

I smile when I read the first words of chapter two, in which angels (including Satan) on another day came to present themselves before the Lord. I wonder how many "on another day" instances have happened since that one spoken about in the book of Job. How many on "other days" had conversations about each of us that we know nothing about and never will? Nothing happens outside of the eyes and will of God.

Recently I listened intently to a new friend from Haiti expressing from different vantage points the unique concept that going through problems and suffering in life should be seen as one of the highlights of living. In other words, issues are a "thrill' or challenges for the journey. Maybe in the future I will have a chance to continue the conversation, but I began to consider if that same viewpoint holds if God allows my friend to reach a new level of far more profound suffering and confusion as was permitted for Job.

For some years my favorite hymn has been "Living by Faith," written by James Wells and R. E. Winsett with the music written by J. L. Heath. It says what might be comforting to you today and something you need to hear repeatedly,

> *I care not today what tomorrow may bring,*
> *If shadow or sunshine or rain.*
> *The Lord, I know, ruleth o'er everything,*
> *And all of my worry is vain.*

> *Living by faith in Jesus above;*
> *Trusting, confiding in His great love;*
> *Safe from all harm in His sheltering arm,*
> *I'm living by faith and feel no alarm.*

Tho' tempests may blow and storm clouds arise,
*   Obscuring the brightness of life,*
I'm never alarmed at the overcast skies;
*   The Master looks on at the strife.*

I know that He safely will carry me thro',
*   No matter what evils betide.*
Why should I then care, tho' the tempest may blow,
*   If Jesus walks close to my side?*

Our Lord will return to this earth some sweet day;
*   Our troubles will then all be o'er.*
The Master so gently will lead us away,
*   Beyond that blest heavenly shore.*

3

The Language and Insinuations from Friends Did Not Confuse Job

We will be exposing the following three truths in this chapter. First, Job is charged with sinful behavior and denies the charge of sin boldly (chapters 4–14). Second, the claims of innocence by Job are according to his friends' further evidence of his guilt and impending danger (chapters 15–21). Third, the afflictions of Job are just the kind to come to the one who yields to temptations such as those Job is subject to (chapters 22–31).

The friends of Job make every effort to pin him against a wall of accusation. The twenty-eight chapters covering the charges by the friends of Job were familiar to contemporary cultural and theological thoughts. Some things seem never to change in seasons of human history. We will also discover that the servant Job took the scorns of many as water (Job 34:7).

Recently in a conversation with one of my doctors, she shared about how deeply and negatively affected her emotions are, having to deal with the suffering of other people daily. She indicated that she was very professional in her interactions with patients but felt inner pain about what she has regularly seen over the years. Her journey into medicine had been spurred by seeing a much-loved uncle dying in his mid-thirties from an illness that made no sense in her mind at that time. As she progressed in her formal studies and later hospital placements, she was positively moved to serve other people by seeing how more impoverished people often did not have the same medical benefits as wealthier clients due to insurance shortage and often lack of finances. "Why do people suffer so much?" was a deep cry from her inner being. A lot of us ask the same question far too often. God does care very much for the vulnerable far more than my doctor does.

I believe that ever since Adam and Eve were forced to leave the Garden of Eden (Genesis 3), humankind has been asking why human beings have to suffer so much. People have come up with different answers over the centuries. Remarkably, some explanations seem to remain the same no matter the generation but often in "different clothing."

The wise writer of Ecclesiastes wrote that there is nothing new under the sun. This comment referred mainly to the basic patterns of human beings: "What has been will be again, what has been done will be done again; there is nothing new under the sun" (Ecclesiastes 1:9).

To this day some people still say that one of the primary reasons for the suffering of individual human beings is their specific immoral behavior. The social thought pattern in the days of Job claimed the same.

One of the first things the friends of Job shared with him is that he had sin in his life and that he needed to receive God's forgiveness and thus have a door through which to be relieved from the suffering he was facing.

Remember that another wise Bible writer said, "Before a downfall the heart is haughty, but humility comes before honor. To answer before listening—that is folly and shame. The human spirit can endure in sickness, but a crushed spirit who can bear? The heart of the discerning acquires knowledge, for the ears of the wise seek it out" (Proverbs 18:12–15).

Going through counseling while suffering has some definite overtones, but swallowing some veins of counsel is not always spiritually healthy, and the book of Job gives reliable guidance and consideration on this matter for God's children. Be wise in choosing counselors from the community of faith. Church leaders are to be careful in appointing counselors in the family of God.

One of the many disciplines from Job to emulate is the strength and vigor with which he spoke in defense of his faith in God during hours of verbal condemnation.

A.

Job is charged with sinful behavior and boldly denies the charge *(Chapters 4–14)*

In similar veins throughout chapters 4–14, the "three friends of Job," Eliphaz the Temanite, Bildad the Shuhite, and Zophar the Naamathite, shared the concept that Job had sinned and that this was the reason for his suffering. In this section I will share some of the words spoken by Bildad and the responses by Job.

There is no way to read Job and not identify that there is a mystery when considering the role of suffering. The secret is also a New Testament truth echoed. The apostle Paul says, "By common confession, great is the mystery of godliness [walking while suffering circumstances]" (1 Timothy 3:16 NASB). But the friends of Job are indicating that the mystery is more natural to fathom by looking at the ramifications of sinful behavior.

If Job were okay spiritually, there would be no reason God would not come and give a great miracle of deliverance on behalf of God's child in his difficult situation. Job must be involved in sin and must therefore pay the price, say his friends.

A preacher known as Major Dalton wrote the story of an incident that captured the attention of the world in 2018 and is illustrative for our vein of thought (taken from the article "Be the Miracle"):

> *On June 23 thirteen soccer players ages 11–16, along with their coach, journeyed into a cave in Thailand. They only intended to be inside for one hour when a monsoon flooded the cave entrance. When the families of the young boys found the*

team's bikes and gear outside the cave, they imme-diately went to work to accomplish the impossible: save their children, all of them.

Vern Unsworth, a local cave hobbyist turned expert, was one of the first called in to help. He connected the community to a network of special-ty British SEAL divers who flew in to assess the situation. Unsworth provided a map of the cave system and suggestions on where the boys would probably be.

In an interview on Friday, one of the divers, Rick Stanton, talked about the moment they found the boys alive. "When we departed," he recounted, "all we could think about was how we were going to get them out." They were focused, fortunate, and ul-timately successful. Unsworth's hobby and the SEAL team's training became resources for an improbable rescue, so unlikely that many have called it an act of God.

Unsworth summarized the outcome, "Just to get any of them out alive would have been a miracle. But to get 13 out of 13 won't happen again." He concluded by simply stating, "Biggest miracle ever!" (Major Dalton, "Be the Miracle: God's Super-

natural Work Through Our Natural Abilities,"
contextive.com, July 9, 2018, https://www.con-
textive.org/2018/07/09/be-the-miracle-gods-su-
pernatural-work-through-our-natural-abilities/)

Miracle, according to Miriam Webster, is "a surprising and welcome event that is not explicable by natural or scientific laws and is therefore considered to be the work of a divine agency." C. S. Lewis was more succinct when he described miracles as "interference with Nature by supernatural power" (https://www.preaching.com/sermon-illustrations/be-the-miracle/).

There must have been a similar mind-set among the friends of Job that supernatural power was not coming to support Job. Something must have been keeping away the power of the Almighty. Some people are going to say the same to you without knowing the extent of the circumstances you are facing. Some will claim that you are not telling the whole truth and in doing so will imply negative confidence in your spiritual journey. Do not let others dwarf your spiritual journey as you walk in God's light.

Therefore, we have Bildad agreeing with and supporting his friends [the bold formating in the following verses is added to show main thought patterns]:

Then Bildad the Shuhite replied:

"How long will you say such things?
Your words are a blustering wind.
Does God pervert justice?
Does the Almighty pervert what is right?
When your children sinned against him,
he gave them over to the penalty of their sin.

But if you will seek God earnestly
and plead with the Almighty,
if you are pure and upright,
even now he will rouse himself on your behalf
and restore you to your prosperous state.
Your beginnings will seem humble,
so prosperous will your future be.

Ask the former generation
and find out what their ancestors learned,
for we were born only yesterday and know nothing,
and our days on earth are but a shadow.
Will they not instruct you and tell you?
Will they not bring forth words from their
understanding?
Can papyrus grow tall where there is no marsh?
Can reeds thrive without water?
While still growing and uncut,
they wither more quickly than grass.
Such is the destiny of all who forget God;
so perishes the hope of the godless.

> *What they trust in is fragile;*
> *what they rely on is a spider's web.*
> *They lean on the web, but it gives way;*
> *they cling to it, but it does not hold.*
> *They are like a well-watered plant in the sunshine,*
> *spreading its shoots over the garden;*
> *it entwines its roots around a pile of rocks*
> *and looks for a place among the stones.*
> *But when it is torn from its spot,*
> *that place disowns it and says, 'I never saw you.'*
> *Surely its life withers away,*
> *and from the soil other plants grow.*
>
> *Surely God does not reject one who is blameless*
> *or strengthen the hands of evildoers.*
> *He will yet fill your mouth with laughter*
> *and your lips with shouts of joy.*
> *Your enemies will be clothed in shame,*
> *and the tents of the wicked will be no more."*
> (8:1–22)

Do we see from the reasoning espoused by Bildad some theological thinking that still abounds today? Yes, and here are some:

1. God does not pervert His laws of justice for anyone.

2. When anyone sins against God in this life, some punishment will be received in the present time and space.

3. The laws of God's justice prevail for any of God's children.

4. Sinning in this life as God's child means that the person must seek God earnestly for forgiveness to receive the personal favor of God again.

5. Despite the reputation of Job, there were evil characteristics that were not fooling God.

6. I suggest that the language and insinuations of Bildad and his brethren in chapters 4–14 can be summarized by the words "Surely God does not reject one who is blameless or strengthen the hands of evildoers "(Job 8:20). Therefore, Job was blamed for some unspoken and unidentified sin, and God will not help, strengthen, and deliver the type of person who hides in that type of "spiritual clothes."

7. In today's vernacular the brothers of Job are trying to give a reasonable religious response for why good people often suffer the fate of ridiculous and often unexplainable tragedy.

The servant Job responds knowing that a number of the points made by his friends were typical of "truths" he had also been brought up believing. For the present day, maturing believers in Christ must be open to spiritual growth.

"The greatest spiritual crisis comes when a person has to move a little farther on in his faith than the beliefs he has already accepted" (Oswald Chambers, *My Utmost for His Highest*, September 15 devotional). Stretching our spirituality is the context in which we reflect on some salient comments by Job in response.

Then Job replied:

> *"Indeed, I know that this is true.*
> *But how can mere mortals prove their innocence*
> *before God?"* (9:1–2)

> *"Although I am blameless,*
> *I have no concern for myself;*
> *I despise my own life.*
> *It is all the same; that is why I say,*
> *'He destroys both the blameless and the wicked.'"*
> (9:21–22)

> *"I say to God: Do not declare me guilty,*
> *but tell me what charges you have against me.*
> *Does it please you to oppress me,*
> *to spurn the work of your hands,*
> *while you smile on the plans of the wicked?"*
> (10:2–3)

> *"But this is what you concealed in your heart,*
> *and I know that this was in your mind:*
> *If I sinned, you would be watching me*

and would not let my offense go unpunished.
If I am guilty—woe to me!
Even if I am innocent, I cannot lift my head,
for I am full of shame
and drowned in my affliction." (10:13–15)

"Keep silent and let me speak;
then let come to me what may.
Why do I put myself in jeopardy
and take my life in my hands?
Though he slay me, yet will I hope in him;
I will surely defend my ways to his face.
Indeed, this will turn out for my deliverance,
for no godless person would dare come
before him!
Listen carefully to what I say;
let my words ring in your ears.
Now that I have prepared my case,
I know I will be vindicated.
Can anyone bring charges against me?
If so, I will be silent and die."
(13:13–19, emphasis added)

The following are interpreted responses given by Job.

1. I know that some of what you say is true. How, then, may I adequately respond? (9:2).

2. I am not ashamed of stating that I am blameless (9:21).

3. There are no sinful charges that God lays at my feet. Woe to me if you can find me guilty (10:1–7).

4. In my innocence I am not able to lift my head as I'm drowned in my affliction and full of shame, knowing my physical ailments (10:15).

5. I express my complete faith and total confidence in God without reservation (13:15).

6. Even unto death and all it entails, I will hope in God (13:15).

7. For sure, I know I will be vindicated when my story is all over (13:18).

I thought that one of the best ways of summarizing the spiritual convictions of Job is sharing a poem (previously un-published) by the late saint Iona Corbett-Franklin (a back-bone member of the Springfield Gardens Church of the Nazarene, Queens, New York) that she shared with me. Sister Iona titled the poem "Bountiful Benefits."

> *How can I say thanks to my gracious, loving,*
> *heavenly Father,*
>
> *Who has been my Rock in times of trials, testings,*
> *despair, sorrow, and pain?*

He has been my Shepherd to guide from
my youth—

My Deliverer in times of danger.

He plucked me as a brand from the fire of
destruction—

Restored my soul, established my goings,

So I learned to trust Him and rely on Him
implicitly.

I thank Him for translating me from the
kingdom of Satan

Into the heavenly kingdom of His dear Son,
Jesus Christ,

Daily filled me with bountiful benefits, and

Brought me from darkness to light,

Adopted me into His own family as an heir
of salvation,

Purchased with the blood of the Lamb,

Giving me all spiritual blessings in heavenly
places in Christ

With an inheritance that will not fade away.

What more can I ask for today?

I am happy for the assurance in His Word that no one can pluck me out of His Hand, I am His, and He is mine forever and forever (John 10: 27–29).

B.

The claims of innocence by Job are further evidence of his guilt and impending danger (Chapters 15–21)

The men who are counseling Job are older and have experienced and seen more situations in their lives. "What do you know that we do not know? What insights do you have that we do not have? The gray-haired and the aged are on our side, men even older than your father" (15:9–10).

The servant Job sees these men as filled with error in their comprehension as to what is going on. Here is Job, a drained and physically feeble man but having strong spiritual convictions. Despite his circumstances, Job speaks boldly with the words "I know that my redeemer lives, and that in the end he will stand on the earth. And after my skin has been destroyed, yet in my flesh I will see God; I will see him with my own eyes—I, and not another. How my heart yearns within me!" (19:25–27).

In your spiritual journey today, please be lifted by inner wisdom and not be overcome with the faulty logic of persons who are more experienced than you. Be sure that the "drum major" for your life is guided by God's Word so that you can be wholly faithful to the Lord who lives in you and gives secure wisdom from above.

"Are you going on with Jesus? The way goes through Gethsemane, through the city gate, and 'outside the camp'

(Hebrews 13:13). The way is lonely and goes on until there is no longer even a trace of a footprint to follow—but only the voice saying, 'Follow me' (Matthew 4:19)" (Oswald Chambers, *My Utmost for His Highest*, September 19 devotional).

The apostle Peter tells us how the friends of Job and Job himself ought to be getting on. "Finally, all of you, be like-minded, be sympathetic, love one another, be compassionate and humble" (1 Peter 3:8). But they are not.

Eliphaz covers well the remarks for all his friends in this section with the following statements [bold is added by the author to emphasize the thoughts of the speakers].

Then Eliphaz, the Temanite replied:

> **"Would a wise person answer with empty notions**
> **or fill their belly with the hot east wind?**
> **Would they argue with useless words,**
> **with speeches that have no value?**
> **But you even undermine piety**
> **and hinder devotion to God.**
> **Your sin prompts your mouth;**
> **you adopt the tongue of the crafty.**
> **Your own mouth condemns you, not mine;**
> **your own lips testify against you.**
>
> *Are you the first man ever born?*
> *Were you brought forth before the hills?*
>
> *Do you listen in on God's council?*

Do you have a monopoly on wisdom?
 What do you know that we do not know?
   What insights do you have that we do not have?
The gray-haired and the aged are on our side,
   men even older than your father.
Are God's consolations not enough for you,
   words spoken gently to you?
Why has your heart carried you away,
   and why do your eyes flash,
so that you vent your rage against God
   and pour out such words from your mouth?

What are mortals, that they could be pure,
   or those born of woman, that they could be
righteous?
If God places no trust in his holy ones,
   if even the heavens are not pure in his eyes,
how much less mortals, who are vile and corrupt,
   who drink up evil like water!

Listen to me and I will explain to you;
   let me tell you what I have seen,
 what the wise have declared,
   hiding nothing received from their ancestors
 (to whom alone the land was given
   when no foreigners moved among them):
All his days the wicked man suffers torment,
   the ruthless man through all the years stored up
   for him.

Terrifying sounds fill his ears;
*   when all seems well, marauders attack him.*
He despairs of escaping the realm of darkness;
*   he is marked for the sword.*
He wanders about for food like a vulture;
*   he knows the day of darkness is at hand.*
Distress and anguish fill him with terror;
*   troubles overwhelm him, like a king poised to*
*   attack,*
because he shakes his fist at God
*   and vaunts himself against the Almighty,*
defiantly charging against him
*   with a thick, strong shield.*

Though his face is covered with fat
*   and his waist bulges with flesh,*
he will inhabit ruined towns
*   and houses where no one lives,*
*   houses crumbling to rubble.*
He will no longer be rich and his wealth will not
*   endure,*
*   nor will his possessions spread over the land.*
He will not escape the darkness;
*   a flame will wither his shoots,*
*   and the breath of God's mouth will carry him*
*   away.*
Let him not deceive himself by trusting what is
worthless,

for he will get nothing in return.
Before his time he will wither,
*   and his branches will not flourish.*
He will be like a vine stripped of its unripe grapes,
*   like an olive tree shedding its blossoms.*
For the company of the godless will be barren,
*   and fire will consume the tents of those who love*
bribes.
They conceive trouble and give birth to evil;
*   their womb fashions deceit. "*
(15:1–35)

To summarize, the above words can be appreciated by humans who sincerely acknowledge their frailty and begin thinking of their demise while their bodies suffer. As a result, they start to seek a cause or a reality more significant than the trauma.

Remember: "Simplicity is the secret to seeing things. A saint does not think clearly until a long time passes, but a saint ought to see clearly without any difficulty. You cannot think through spiritual confusion to make things clear; to make things clear, you must obey" (Oswald Chambers, *My Utmost for His Highest*, September 14 devotional).

People who have gone through suffering, (whether physical or emotional) and come out grateful often become better individuals. These are persons who have acquired more patience, courage, understanding, and humility, which are all keys to becoming more like God. The growth of these believers happens mostly as a result of their encounter with their moments of suffering.

According to the friends of Job, the innocent defense by Job is further evidence of his guilt and is a security warning sign of more significant impending danger ahead for him. Their "distortive wisdom" is compelling for debate but inaccurate regarding Job.

The following are direct responses by the servant of Job in his limited understanding of the broader circumstances he is facing; but the physical pain felt is as profound as the night that follows the day. It is a dark corner to be in when a friend tells you that your sin is causing your mouth to say false statements and your mouth condemns you (15:5–6).

Then Job replied:

> *"How long will you torment me*
> *and crush me with words?*
> *Ten times now you have reproached me;*
> *shamelessly you attack me.*
> *If it is true that I have gone astray,*
> *my error remains my concern alone.*
> *If indeed you would exalt yourselves above me*
> *and use my humiliation against me,*
> *then know that God has wronged me*
> *and drawn his net around me.*

Though I cry, 'Violence!' I get no response;
  though I call for help, there is no justice.
He has blocked my way so I cannot pass;
  he has shrouded my paths in darkness.
He has stripped me of my honor
  and removed the crown from my head."
  (19:1–9)

"Listen carefully to my words;
  let this be the consolation you give me.
Bear with me while I speak,
  and after I have spoken, mock on.

Is my complaint directed to a human being?
  Why should I not be impatient?
Look at me and be appalled;
  clap your hand over your mouth.
When I think about this, I am terrified;
  trembling seizes my body.
Why do the wicked live on,
  growing old and increasing in power?
They see their children established around them,
  their offspring before their eyes.
Their homes are safe and free from fear;
  the rod of God is not upon them."
  (21:2–9)

"I know full well what you are thinking,
*   the schemes by which you would wrong me.*
You say, 'Where now is the house of the great,
*   the tents where the wicked lived?'*
Have you never questioned those who travel?
*   Have you paid no regard to their accounts—*
that the wicked are spared from the day of
*   calamity,*
*   that they are delivered from the day of wrath?*
Who denounces their conduct to their face?
*   Who repays them for what they have done?*
They are carried to the grave,
*   and watch is kept over their tombs. The soil in*
the valley is sweet to them;
*   everyone follows after them,*
*   and a countless throng goes before them.*

So how can you console me with your nonsense?
*   Nothing is left of your answers but falsehood!"*
(21:27–34)

I am anticipating that some people reading this book may never have understood the conversations between Job and his so-called friends fruitfully. Don't knock yourself. It is not too late to make an effort at this season in your life. First, let's be honest and admit that many friendships we have are complicated. We see this portrayed in movies and television series, and you can attest to it in your family relationships and church families if you have the benefit of those relationships.

When in an intimate relationship with our Lord, one of the most important truths to glean from the book of Job is his singular focus no matter the convoluted logic that the friends are advocating. I have a strong feeling that many readers are asking over and over again why God "sits back" and allows spiritually incorrect conversations to continue among well-meaning brothers and sisters. In chapter 6 I will share a few comments about the timing permitted by God.

I am sure it is dangerous for us believers to become settled and complacent in our present levels of spiritual experiences. The Christian life requires preparation and even more preparation in our journey for all growing brothers and sisters in Christ.

You are right. I am saying that for most of the characters in this book (except the devil) there is a God-designed growing drama for the individuals. It is the intention of the Holy Spirit that many of us will be challenged to grow in our shameless audacity to love and be committed to Jesus Christ all the days of our lives.

In concluding this section of the book of Job, the servant highlights the following in responding to friends:

1. My pain is magnified by the repeated crushing words you throw at me (19:1–4).

2. Many wealthy people with ungodly lives seemingly do not suffer, and it often makes no sense to other people looking on (21:2–9).

3. Your "consolation" is unwise because you do not appreciate that I am spiritually blameless in the eyes of our God, and that gives me freedom despite my pain and confusion. "Nothing is left of your answers but falsehood!" (21:34).

I believe I understand a little of what Job went through. In early 2017 I faced a letter sent by a few brethren I had nurtured and served for years as their pastor. This letter was filled with numerous misrepresentations about me and my ministry. It happened at about the time when my physical ailments were leading me toward my resignation in a few months, but it hastened my departure. I mention this fact for only one reason. Sometimes in the journey of life when it looks as if life has given the worst, there is even more darkness behind the corner.

The bad news is that the most significant pain can come from people you love and admire the most. I refer here to my church brothers and sisters and leaders who have often felt closer than blood family. When the church family seems to forget and wounds the already-wounded Christian even more, the God of grace is there and is abundant in His love.

If only "the blood of suffering" were mine alone. Unfortunately, suffering often affects people in our own homes. The two daughters God gave us are miracles from birth. Ann and I married in 1980, and for twelve years we were not able to have children, and then God gave us two beautiful children. The most painful sacrifice made while church planting is often not having a stable church structure as Ann and I had growing up in the Church of the Nazarene. We believe what the wise man says: "Start children off on the way they should go, and even when they are old they will not turn from it" (Proverbs 22:6), and we have taught and lived Christ before our kids.

Our girls have seen spiritually unattractive behavior in some people within our faith, and it has disabled their confidence in our church. I do not know how far or long they will stay away from our denomination. The pain of suffering is real and can haunt. One's pain or pitfall is not the end of the story for anyone in God's favor. God will honor the consequences of our obedience in the lives of others.

C.

The afflictions of Job are just the kind to come to the one who yields to temptations such as those Job is subject to
(*Chapters 22–31*)

The gist of these ten chapters is the implication that Job has given in to temptations and entered the traps of sin according to the counselors of Job. The results of falling from the favor of God have led to the enormous afflictions borne by the patriarch Job. The servant of God refutes this mind-set and the conclusions of his "empty-words friends" (Job 16:3).

The apostle Paul says in 1 Corinthians 10:13, "No temptation has overtaken you except what is common to mankind." As I have reflected on this holy book, was not Job also tempted by unholy concepts during his afflicted days, and wasn't this compounded by the misguided counseling sessions of friends? As a human being Job must have, because temptation (which is the other side of the same coin, called "testings") comes to every human being. Facing these obstacles is a part of the sovereignty and economy of our Lord and Master. Nowhere do we see Job lusting for an immediate answer from God, but he sought the King of Kings from a broken and tender heart.

Dealing with temptation is not sin—it is an experience everyone meets, including the man Job, by merely being a part of the human family. Facing temptations/testings is precisely what the Bible teaches in its totality. Temptation becomes sin only when the person chooses in thoughts, words, and deeds to willingly follow the pathway that the attraction urges him or her to pursue.

You may not want to hear it, but temptations are not something any of us can escape; in fact, it is essential and bedrock for overcoming in the growing and well-rounded

Christian person. The servant Job went through what was the common inheritance of the human family. Job in his walk of faith endured temptations among the testing that started at the very highest levels.

God sustains in temptations whoever will exhibit shameless audacity in his or her intimacy with God. The afflictions that Job faced were not a result of yielding to temptations. You and I know that truth because we have read the beginning of the book, and Job was blinded as to how it started—but not spiritually blind in his high confidence and love for God.

The story of how Jesus overcame His temptations/testing in the wilderness experience as recorded in Matthew 4:1–11 provides a message to anyone who will follow the way of the cross. We read,

> *Then Jesus was led by the Spirit into the wilderness to be tempted by the devil. After fasting forty days and forty nights; he was hungry. The tempter came to him and said, "If you are the Son of God, tell these stones to become bread."*
>
> *Jesus answered, "It is written: 'Man shall not live on bread alone, but on every word that comes from the mouth of God.'"*
>
> *Then the devil took him to the holy city and had him stand on the highest point of the temple. "If you are the Son of God," he said, "throw yourself down. For it is written:*

"'He will command his angels concerning you, and they will lift you up in their hands, so that you will not strike your foot against a stone.'"

Jesus answered him, "It is also written: 'Do not put the Lord your God to the test.'"

Again, the devil took him to a very high mountain and showed him all the kingdoms of the world and their splendor. "All this I will give you," he said, "if you will bow down and worship me."

Jesus said to him, "Away from me, Satan! For it is written: 'Worship the Lord your God, and serve him only.'"

Then the devil left him, and angels came and attended him.

The same triumphant bulwark used by Jesus to overcome temptations throughout his life is the same bulwark that was used by Job and must be copied by any of us who take the way of Christian faith seriously. It means we journey in "thick and in thin" and overcome through the presence of God the Holy Spirit (Matthew 4:1), the Word of God (Matthew 4:4, 7, 10), and total commitment or shameless audacity loving and obeying God. This way of victory and obedient living led Jesus to the cross to die for the sins of the whole world.

Jesus's blood, shed on the cross, washes anyone who will plunge by faith into His blood; and He rose from the dead on the third day to give resurrection power and a holy lifestyle to God's family members.

An excellent way to express the intimacy of the loving relationship between Job and his Lord is using words by the beloved toward her lover in the book Song of Songs: "I am my beloved's and my beloved is mine. . . . I belong to my beloved, and his desire is for me" (Song of Songs 6:3; 7:10).

The three staples to overcoming temptation previously mentioned give the framework for the triumphant lifestyle of Jesus and are the same used by Job in overcoming the negative interactive conversations with his friends. Like you, I will never meet Eliphaz, Bildad, and Zophar in this life. The last of the three gentlemen spoke less in the comments recorded and gave the impression of being more reserved. Zophar may have listened more, but his remarks indicated the same trend of thinking as his friends. Despite being the least vocal of the three, Zophar had elements of the harshest comments to Job. Please note that in this book I have referred only to quotes from Eliphaz and Bildad, but this is not an indication that what was said by Zophar had any less meaning.

Then Eliphaz the Temanite replied:

> "Can a man be of benefit to God?
> Can even a wise person benefit him?

What pleasure would it give the Almighty if you
were righteous?
   What would he gain if your ways were
   blameless?

Is it for your piety that he rebukes you
   and brings charges against you?
Is not your wickedness great?
   Are not your sins endless?

[In other words, the servant Job has fallen into sin due to giving in to temptations and breaking the laws of God.]

You demanded security from your relatives for no
reason;
   you stripped people of their clothing, leaving
them naked.
You gave no water to the weary
   and you withheld food from the hungry,
though you were a powerful man, owning land—
   an honored man, living on it.
And you sent widows away empty-handed
   and broke the strength of the fatherless.
That is why snares are all around you,
   why sudden peril terrifies you,
why it is so dark you cannot see,

and why a flood of water covers you."
(22:1–11)

[In plain English, Job is being told that he has yielded to temptations, and it only follows logically that your suffering is the fitting end to a lifestyle of covered-up sins that have displeased God.]

Then Bildad the Shuhite replied:

"Dominion and awe belong to God;
    he establishes order in the heights of heaven.
Can his forces be numbered?
    On whom does his light not rise?
How then can a mortal be righteous before God?
    How can one born of woman be pure?
If even the moon is not bright
    and the stars are not pure in his eyes,
how much less a mortal, who is but a maggot—
    a human being, who is only a worm!"
(25:1–6)

[Specifically, every human being must fall to temptation at some time, say the friends of Job, and this has happened to you, Job—you are now paying the price.]

As you read Job's response to his friends, he does speak voluminously in these ten chapters of our focus. Also, Job does guard his tongue against falling into spiritual negativity. To emphasize the thought pattern of God's servant, the scripture says,

And Job continued his discourse:

> *"As surely as God lives, who has denied me justice,*
> *the Almighty, who has made my life bitter,*
> *as long as I have life within me,*
> *the breath of God in my nostrils,*
> *my lips will not say anything wicked,*
> *and my tongue will not utter lies.*
> *I will never admit you are in the right;*
> *till I die, I will not deny my integrity.*
> *I will maintain my innocence and never*
> *let go of it;*
> *my conscience will not reproach me as long as*
> *I live."*
>
> (27:1–6)

Testing can become a temptation that we must overcome by the grace of God. Many persons have lived the patient Christian life victoriously in Christ. You and I can do the same. These challenging times for Job are intended to foster spiritual growth for persons today who look on with a heart that wants to learn continuously and succeed in their spiritual journey for the glory of God.

If any of us lives any length of time as servants of Christ, we will have seasons of suffering and far too often seemingly unnecessary pain. Like you, I have shed my tears in the night season. Many other servants of old lived lives of profound patience. This book is a challenge to us to live in victory in Christ and enjoy overcoming lives just like Job.

The book of James is the only place in the New Testament in which there is a mention of Job (5:11). The servant Job was a blessed man who lived a life not only of earthly riches and provisions but also one of vibrant faith in God. Keep remembering that our Lord allowed Job to suffer for a season to grow his soul in his relationship with God.

Job faced days of serious inner questioning, doubt, great hurt, discouragement, and loss of respect, material possessions, and health. Later in this book you will see the testimony of Job that proclaimed the vision he had received to unlock continued victory in that season of his life.

As his personal defense to his friends, Job is quoted in the following and exhibits authority and power in his convictions.

> "But if I go to the east, he is not there;
>   if I go to the west, I do not find him.
> When he is at work in the north, I do not see him;
>   when he turns to the south, I catch no glimpse
>   of him.

But he knows the way that I take;
  when he has tested me, I will come forth as gold.
My feet have closely followed his steps;
  I have kept to his way without turning aside.
I have not departed from the commands of his lips;
  I have treasured the words of his mouth more
than my daily bread."

(23:8–12)

And Job continued his discourse:

"As surely as God lives, who has denied me justice,
  the Almighty, who has made my life bitter,
as long as I have life within me,
  the breath of God in my nostrils,
my lips will not say anything wicked,
  and my tongue will not utter lies.
I will never admit you are in the right;
  till I die, I will not deny my integrity.
I will maintain my innocence and never
  let go of it;
  my conscience will not reproach me as long as
I live."

(27:1–6)

"How I long for the months gone by,
  for the days when God watched over me,

when his lamp shone on my head
    and by his light I walked through darkness!
Oh, for the days when I was in my prime,
    when God's intimate friendship blessed
    my house,
when the Almighty was still with me
    and my children were around me,
when my path was drenched with cream
    and the rock poured out for me streams
    of olive oil.

"When I went to the gate of the city
    and took my seat in the public square,
the young men saw me and stepped aside
    and the old men rose to their feet;
the chief men refrained from speaking
    and covered their mouths with their hands;
the voices of the nobles were hushed,
    and their tongues stuck to the roof of
    their mouths.
Whoever heard me spoke well of me,
    and those who saw me commended me,
because I rescued the poor who cried for help,
    and the fatherless who had none to assist them."
    (29:2–12)

"I made a covenant with my eyes
    not to look lustfully at a young woman.

For what is our lot from God above,
   our heritage from the Almighty on high?
Is it not ruin for the wicked,
   disaster for those who do wrong?
Does he not see my ways
   and count my every step?

If I have walked with falsehood
   or my foot has hurried after deceit—
let God weigh me in honest scales
   and he will know that I am blameless—

if my steps have turned from the path,
   if my heart has been led by my eyes,
   or if my hands have been defiled,
then may others eat what I have sown,
   and may my crops be uprooted."
   (31:1–8)

In concluding this particular conversation, I am driven to note Christian interaction that I believe is not taught or preached about enough or mentioned sufficiently to suffering people. I do not know the biblical duration for the physical, emotional, and psychological suffering endured by the patriarch Job. I lean toward the thinking that the suffering period recorded may not have been more than several months or was perhaps roughly one year (this remains another unanswered question). But whatever the length of suffering, the intensity and depth of the suffering person are the focus here.

Satan did his worse with Job within what was allowed by God. Remember: there are experiences in life that seem worse than death. What can we "hide in our hearts" to uphold the person who lives with ongoing and very stubborn testing/temptation especially fostered by family members, sexual difficulties, money problems, in-law provocations, and the hurts promoted by so-called friends?

I suggest three truths to soberly reflect on. I believe the following is an accurate interpretive lens that helps complement the study the book of Job.

First, Jesus heals a man born blind:

> As he went along, he saw a man blind from birth. His disciples asked him, "Rabbi, who sinned, this man or his parents, that he was born blind?"
>
> "Neither this man nor his parents sinned," said Jesus, "but this happened so that the works of God might be displayed in him. As long as it is day, we must do the works of him who sent me. Night is coming, when no one can work. While I am in the world, I am the light of the world."
>
> After saying this, he spit on the ground, made some mud with the saliva, and put it on the man's eyes. "Go," he told him, "wash in the Pool of Siloam" (this word means "Sent"). So the man went and washed, and came home seeing.
>
> (John 9:1–7)

There are situations in life that God allows or ordains that make sense only to God. We walk by faith, says the Bible (2 Corinthians 5:7). When you're dealing with prolonged suffering, wait on God's overarching comprehension and intervention; please do not quit in your shameless audacity in your love for and confidence in God.

Some burdens carried by people make sense only to God on this side of eternity. Friends, please give those burdens to God. Allow Him to crucify anything in you that rivals His control of your life. Offer a spiritual sacrifice to God; "offer your bodies as a living sacrifice" (Romans 12:1).

Second, remember the apostle Paul repeatedly asking God to heal him of a personal physical ailment that brought suffering and pain to him. The answer he received was "'My grace is sufficient for you, for my power is made perfect in weakness.' Therefore, I will boast all the more gladly about my weaknesses, so that Christ's power may rest on me" (2 Corinthians 12:9).

You may hear some preachers and teachers say to others or you that God is not healing you because you do not have enough faith in Jesus. This message is not authoritative. Keep praying, but rely on Paul's experience mentioned for a better answer when God seems not to be answering your prayer. Although you may be spiritually weak, be utterly open to allowing our gracious God to fulfill the promise and confidence expressed in 2 Corinthians 12:9.

Third, brother or sister reading, there may be some situations that are so deeply painful and complex that you need to share them with a professional Christian counselor for intervention. Sometimes receiving professional counseling may be necessary for enhancing your victory with Jesus in your daily walk.

Also consider counselors, teachers, and other Christian professionals. The apostle James writes, "Dear brothers and sisters, not many of you should become teachers in the church, for we who teach will be judged more strictly. Indeed, we all make many mistakes. For if we could control our tongues, we would be perfect and could also control ourselves in every other way" (James 3:1–2 NLT).

The reality of your life is factual, but please do not jump to the wrong conclusions. Whatever your situation, it is essential not to fall into spiritual dejection or lean toward a "give up" spirit. When it appears that God has not answered your prayer, you are prone to melancholy. Keep a robust spiritual focus and seek God foremostly, who gives all the answers. God is never late or forgets. Do not try to force the hand of God. Dejection is a sign of spiritual illness and needs to be dealt with by the rational conclusions you determine based on God's Word and the promises and assurances He gives to His children.

4

The Lips of Elihu Speak with
Contempt to Job
(Chapters 32–37)

If you think Eliphaz, Bildad, and Zophar have been "a royal pain" while conversing with Job during this horrible time of his life—you are right. However, when I read the following verses, which act as a transition to a sermon-type presentation by Elihu, I smile considering the arrogance exhibited at times by this younger man. Youth often has no fear, but it does not mean that wisdom is attached to every action taken by younger people. Be aware that the words spoken by Elihu could well be a voice for the mind-set of some immature people in our churches:

> *So these three men stopped answering Job because he was righteous in his own eyes. But Elihu son of Barakel the Buzite, of the family of Ram, became very angry with Job for justifying himself rather than God. He was also angry with the three friends, because they had found no way to refute Job, and yet had condemned him. Now Elihu had waited before speaking to Job because they were*

older than he. But when he saw that the three men
had nothing more to say, his anger was aroused.
(32:1–5)

The apostle James in the New Testament says, "Who is wise and understanding among you? By his good conduct he should show his works done in the gentleness that wisdom brings" (James 3:13 NET). We live in a culture and environment that is constantly attacking and undermining right living for God. Of course, it was also true in the days of Job (some things never change). Elihu is supporting the arguments of the three persons who have been making accusations against Job, but he feels that Eliphaz, Bildad, and Zophar have come up short in being sufficiently convincing and searching.

Recently while I was looking for a simple paper clip that I knew I had put down. For a while I could not locate the clip, but after a few minutes of dealing with the mystery, I noticed that it had been right in front of me all the time. What I am saying is that we can too easily be looking at the forest while often missing one crucial tree. What is Elihu speaking?

One of the truths about the book of Job that is quickly lost is the fact that some of the things said by the friends of the patriarch are sometimes true in principle and applicable for other people in the world even to this day. What I am saying is this:

1. Some people suffer today in ways that are a result of past sinful behaviors.

2. The claims of innocence by some people claiming to be Christians are not correct but are further evidence of their guilt and impending danger. Pretense does not fool God.

3. The afflictions of some well-meaning people are just the kind to come to the one who has yielded to temptation and living a bad life.

Elihu seems to be stating that the previous truths have not been pinned strong enough on the life of Job. As such, the new speaker, Elihu, felt he knew better ways to hold Job against the wall of accusation. As you suffer today, you may have people like Elihu enter your life. First you need to be honest with yourself about the character and integrity of your relationship with God. Do you need to confess now to sinful things in your life? Do you need to completely repent for your sins, which pull your soul away from God, and trust Jesus? It is always appropriate to do some honest heart-searching and surrender all to Jesus.

The following are a few statements on the subject of wisdom. Christian wisdom is practical, especially the knowledge that God gives to His children. An influential Christian and holy leader lives a kind and gentle life. Sense starts at the very core of our being and our attitudes. Remember: human reason is prone to lead to confusion and wickedness in relationships. I love James 3:16–18 because it is similar to the critical journey that speaks about the fruit of the Spirit in Galatians 5:22–25. James says, "For where you have envy and selfish ambition, there you find disorder and every evil practice. But the wisdom that comes from heaven is first of all pure; then peace-loving, considerate, submissive, full of mercy and good fruit, impartial and sincere. Peacemakers who sow in peace reap a harvest of righteousness."

Maybe there is someone who knows the experience of saying, "I'm tired, dear Lord"—meaning tired of the pain in my body, of the injustice being meted out, of having so little, of saying "amen" in a church family that does not understand how much I am hurting, of shedding tears that do not seem to move the heart of God, of people who say they care. You may also be thinking like the writer when he said, "But as for me, my feet had almost slipped; I had nearly lost my foothold. For I envied the arrogant when I saw the prosperity of the wicked. They have no struggles; their bodies are healthy and strong. They are free from common human burdens; they are not plagued by human ills"(Psalm 73:2–5).

Job in his unique way is saying to his three friends and Elihu, "But as for me, it is good to be near God. I have made the Sovereign Lord my refuge" (Psalm 73:28).

I wonder how Elihu and the three other men who spoke to Job would have responded to the words of the apostle Paul to the church in Galatia about a hurting and fallen brother or sister. Paul writes,

> *Brothers and sisters, if someone is caught in a sin, you who live by the Spirit should restore that person gently. But watch yourselves, or you also may be tempted. Carry each other's burdens, and in this way, you will fulfill the law of Christ. If anyone thinks they are something when they are not, they deceive themselves. Each one should test their own actions. Then they can take pride in themselves alone, without comparing themselves to someone else, for each one should carry their own load. Nevertheless, the one who receives instruction in the word should share all good things with their instructor.*
>
> *Do not be deceived: God cannot be mocked. A man reaps what he sows. Whoever sows to please their flesh, from the flesh will reap destruction; whoever sows to please the Spirit, from the Spirit will reap eternal life. Let us not become weary in doing good, for at the proper time we will reap a harvest if we do not give up. Therefore, as we have opportunity, let us do good to all people, especially to those who belong to the family of believers.* (Galatians 6:1–10)

When Job 32:1 says of Job, "He was righteous in his own eyes," we know it was speaking not of a self-righteous and pious expression but one that came from a God-given personal assurance that all was at peace with God. Our Lord wants to give that same assurance to every person who has genuinely left all of his or her sins in genuine repentance at the foot of the cross and put his or her faith in Christ alone for salvation from sin. Remember: Job's righteousness was confirmed in the heavenly realm also because at the beginning of the book of Job, God testified to it.

One thing to love about Elihu is the fact that he was confident in his faith as a younger person in comparison to others. I hope some of the people who read this book are younger (and many young people also suffer in ways parents and friends sometimes do not appreciate). The sad reality is that hopelessness and suicide levels continue at alarming levels among the young. Hope and victory are available for the young in the midst of their pain and suffering.

Young people can be the most shamelessly audacious in their walk of faith with Jesus. When I was younger it was said by church elders that we are to be sold out to God's will for our lives. That is holy living. A life of holiness is accepting the call to be addicted to Jesus and being filled each moment of each day with the Holy Ghost. Let's teach well in our churches that young men and women must treat each other with moral purity and not be found with any traces of immorality.

Paul the apostle, says, "Don't let anyone look down on you because you are young, but set an example for the believers in speech, in conduct, in love, in faith and in purity" (1 Timothy 4:12).

The enthusiasm with which Elihu shared his thoughts is seen in the following:

> *"I too will have my say;*
> *I too will tell what I know.*
> *For I am full of words,*
> *and the spirit within me compels me;*
> *inside I am like bottled-up wine,*
> *like new wineskins ready to burst.*
> *I must speak and find relief;*
> *I must open my lips and reply.*
>
> *I will show no partiality,*
> *nor will I flatter anyone;*
> *for if I were skilled in flattery,*
> *my Maker would soon take me away."*
> (32:17–22)

In the thirty-third chapter of Job I note the maturity shown the young man about how much greater God is, versus humankind in diverse ways, and in the pointed ways He deals with and speaks to human beings. When the Lord speaks, He intends to help us to be in a complete restorative and redemptive relationship with God.

It is within the body of chapter 34 that Elihu begins to lose sight of truths that are bigger than him:

Then Elihu said:

> *"Hear my words, you wise men;*
>> *listen to me, you men of learning.*
> *For the ear tests words*
>> *as the tongue tastes food.*
> *Let us discern for ourselves what is right;*
>> *let us learn together what is good.*
>
> *Job says, 'I am innocent,*
>> *but God denies me justice.*
> *Although I am right,*
>> *I am considered a liar;*
> *although I am guiltless,*
>> *his arrow inflicts an incurable wound.'*
> *Is there anyone like Job,*
>> *who drinks scorn like water?*
> *He keeps company with evildoers;*
>> *he associates with the wicked.*
> *For he says, 'There is no profit*
>> *in trying to please God.'*
>
> *So listen to me, you men of understanding.*
>> *Far be it from God to do evil,*
>> *from the Almighty to do wrong.*
> *He repays everyone for what they have done;*
>> *he brings on them what their conduct deserves.*

It is unthinkable that God would do wrong,
  that the Almighty would pervert justice.
Who appointed him over the earth?
  Who put him in charge of the whole world?
If it were his intention
  and he withdrew his spirit and breath,

all humanity would perish together
  and mankind would return to the dust."
  (34:1–15)

Unfortunately, the speaker utters that Job has secret sins:

"Should God then reward you on your terms,
when you refuse to repent? You must decide, not I; so
tell me what you know. Men of understanding de-
clare, wise men who hear me say to me, 'Job speaks
without knowledge; his words lack insight.' Oh,
that Job might be tested to the utmost for answering
like a wicked man! To his sin he adds rebellion."
  (34:33–37)

Like previous accusers, Elihu does not know the back story to Job's life, but he is trying to be honest in his evaluation. For those who are walking with God and suffering, keep remembering that comments sometimes made by well-meaning individuals are limited in what is actually going on with your life.

A wiser old saint mentioned before (Iona Corbett-Franklin) wrote a poem to be remembered by youth and growing children:

> You are one of God's precious jewels
>   Etched in gold.
> You were born with lots of potential
>   That cannot be bought or sold.
> So as you grow from year to year,
>   May your life be as a garden fair
> With love, joy, peace, and kindness
>   Springing up everywhere,
> Spreading beautiful sunshine and cheer
>   As God's happy messenger.

Remember that the Word of the Lord says, "Let those who love the Lord hate evil, for he guards the lives of his faithful ones and delivers them from the hand of the wicked" (Psalm 97:10).

It is my personal belief that Elihu would have enjoyed hearing the following truths from the gospel of John. I hope each reader will pause and reflect also: "Everyone who does evil hates the light, and will not come into the light for fear that their deeds will be exposed. But whoever lives by the truth comes into the light, so that it may be seen plainly that what they have done has been done in the sight of God" (John 3:20–21.)

As a transition into our next chapter, the words by Elihu open the doors to the Lord's directly speaking and making revelation to Job. We are now facing exposure to the greatness of God from different vantage points through His creation.

> *"Listen to this, Job;*
> *stop and consider God's wonders.*
> *Do you know how God controls the clouds*
> *and makes his lightning flash?*
> *Do you know how the clouds hang poised,*
> *those wonders of him who has perfect knowledge?*
> *You who swelter in your clothes*
> *when the land lies hushed under the south wind,*
> *can you join him in spreading out the skies,*
> *hard as a mirror of cast bronze?"*
> (37:14–18)

5

The Lord's Revelation to Job
(Chapters 38–41)

God now has a very frank discussion with Job. We are at another life-transforming point for the servant Job. These four chapters are one the best exponents of the general revelation of God's creation that exposes the heart and loving care of our heavenly Father for every detail of His nature.

As God cares for everything on this earth and all other creation is second to the value of a human soul, we should take particular note. These chapters are the background for the healing and restoring of Job from his suffering plight.

Remember that Jesus said in Matthew 5:11–12, "Blessed are you when people insult you, persecute you and falsely say all kinds of evil against you because of me. Rejoice and be glad, because great is your reward in heaven, for in the same way they persecuted the prophets who were before you."

Sometimes we as God's children have moments and seasons of inspiration in our journey through life. But God never allows any of us to stay in the cloud of motivation because we have a world filled with valleys we need to face and be channels of Christ-like love to others who are very needy even when we are suffering and facing challenges.

Keep in mind always that it is the low times of life (during your suffering, pain, trials, and mundane experiences) when you must learn to live best for the glory of Jesus Christ. As a disciple of Christ, you are His light regardless of the circumstances in which find yourself.

Chapters 38–41 were a learning season for Job in interacting with God—and also a tremendous refreshing season after so much pain and havoc. Why had God been silent for so long as Job remained swamped with so much inaccuracy? Do you realize that God's silence is often a special privilege for some of you since it means that our Savior has trusted you with His silence, which will bring Him glory?

Remember the story of Lazarus and his sisters—all were friends of Jesus, as recorded in John 11. In John 11:4–7 it is registered regarding hearing that Lazarus was very sick, "When he heard this, Jesus said, 'This sickness will not end in death. No, it is for God's glory so that God's Son may be glorified through it.' Now Jesus loved Martha and her sister and Lazarus. So when he heard that Lazarus was sick, he stayed where he was two more days, and then he said to his disciples, 'Let us go back to Judea.'"

Why was God silent for so long with this family in their time of need? Jesus was allowing them to be a part of one of the most significant miracles in the New Testament. Jesus had so much confidence with this family's faith that He did nothing for a few days and said nothing. The Lord revealed heavenly blessing in His silence when God was keeping quiet and merely observing. It takes a shameless audacity in our love for God for Him to trust us enough with His silence.

Likewise, God had listened enough to the conversations between Job and the men who had gathered with him. The servant Job was swamped with gross innuendoes and speculations that were far from the truth. But guess what—even Job was not always seeing clearly as evidenced by some of his statements that fell short of the mark. God helped to open the eyes of Job by asking him over sixty direct questions that Job could not answer, causing him to be genuinely amazed and stunned. Through this questioning encounter Job received a dose of "revelation sense."

In Job 12:7–10 Job had indicated that animals could be a source of unraveling the "suffering mysteries" he had faced. The questions by God now focused on His creation and handiwork, and these were holy moments for Job. Indeed, the servant of the Lord was standing on "holy ground" in these chapters.

In 1953 Stuart Hine wrote the words and music for the great hymn "How Great Thou Art." Psalm 86:10 says, "You are great and do marvelous deeds; you alone are God," and is used to give scriptural support for the great lyrics, but God's whole conversation with Job could well have used as the scriptural support for this hymn for all generations. Look up the lyrics and reflect on them.

The personal impact on Job from conversations with God is summed up in his own words in 40:3–5: "Then Job answered the Lord: 'I am unworthy—how can I reply to you? I put my hand over my mouth. I spoke once, but I have no answer—twice, but I will say no more.'" In these verses we see Job openly acknowledging his brokenness and a limited appreciation of the whole, and this will not be the last time seen in this excellent book. What was the context for the remarks of Job will be a key for unlocking what we are examining.

Job in his suffering, sickness, and pain was seeking answers and a better appreciation as to why his life had come apart. From the conversations we have seen with his friends, Job must have wondered why his relationships had gone downhill so tragically and so fast. Where was God in all he was facing? Had divine purpose gone haywire? As we look at the gambit of the Scriptures, Job was not alone in his journey and challenges. Remember how King David opined in a time of his struggles in Psalm 40:1–3:

> *I waited patiently for the Lord;*
> *he turned to me and heard my cry.*
> *He lifted me out of the slimy pit,*
> *out of the mud and mire;*
> *he set my feet on a rock*
> *and gave me a firm place to stand.*

He put a new song in my mouth,
a hymn of praise to our God.
Many will see and fear the Lord
and put their trust in him.

I admonish all readers to reflect again on the lyrics of the hymn of praise "How Great Thou Art." Stop and sing if you have the know-how and can. Sometimes in our low days in our valleys, the only way to shamelessly and audaciously express our love for God is to sing or listen to God-glorifying music while going through hellish days. Always remember that Jesus loves you supremely and that you can never face or think of something that has never been considered previously by our Lord. It is not the time or season to give into fretting and worry (meditate on Matthew 7:11).

Without shame, I confess the joyful comfort and refreshing that often come to my soul playing Christian songs in my room and allowing the glory of the Lord to fill my being. Imagine my trying to "dance unto the Lord" too in response to upbeat music played for my heart, which has been made pure by the blood of Jesus and blameless in His sight. If you can dance unto the Lord some days, be encouraged to do so. Hallelujah!

The salvation of our Lord in us will sustain His children as He did Job. If and when you seem to be going through Hell, do not stop and wallow in self-pity and hopelessness, but keep pushing forward, trusting entirely in Jesus and the power of the cross. You might need to learn to laugh again, sing again, and dance on your Christian journey, even if you have been suffering some sad days.

Many Bible heroes knew the joy of God's grace and were lifted higher because they endured difficult circumstances and times of suffering. The cross is the symbolic center of the Bible through the life, death, and resurrection of Jesus Christ. Our Savior gives hope to whosoever will receive Him as fallen and broken human beings. Remember: "Weeping may stay for the night, but rejoicing comes in the morning" (Psalm 30:5). Sadness is a significant part of the story of Job. God uses pain to shape a better central character for the servant of God in this book. He wants to do the same for each reader.

"Then the Lord spoke to Job out of the storm" (Job 38:1). "Where did a real storm come from?" some may ask. I believe the original language of the scripture and common sense will help us appreciate that the writer is speaking allegorically in referring to the storm or whirlwind. Please understand this turning point in the book and focus on the importance of this intense scene. The majesty and glory of God's presence are wholly different from the human inadequacies that had taken place in previous social conversations.

"Job, you have indicated knowing the more profound things of God—now it is My time to challenge you," God says. "Put on your best mind and understanding and answer Me like a man." Wow!

Among the over sixty questions that God asks Job, these are included:

> *"What is the way to the abode of light?*
> *And where does darkness reside?*
> *Can you take them to their places?*
> *Do you know the paths to their dwellings?*
> *Surely you know, for you were already born!*
> *You have lived so many years!"*
> (38:18–21)

You and your friends who are so mature and have lived so long and experienced so much; please tell me the origins of light and darkness! Job is stunned.

> *"Do you know when the mountain*
> *goats give birth?*
> *Do you watch when the doe bears her fawn?*
> *Do you count the months till they bear?*
> *Do you know the time they give birth?*
> *They crouch down and bring forth their young;*
> *their labor pains are ended.*
> *Their young thrive and grow strong in the wilds;*
> *they leave and do not return."*
> (39:1–4)

Come on, Job—tell me about what happened to the mama mountain goats and what happened to their kids. You seem to know more about the details of God's creation. The man Job is overwhelmed.

> "The wings of the ostrich flap joyfully,
>   though they cannot compare
>   with the wings and feathers of the stork.
> She lays her eggs on the ground
>   and lets them warm in the sand,
> unmindful that a foot may crush them,
>   that some wild animal may trample them.
> She treats her young harshly, as if they were
>   not hers;
>   she cares not that her labor was in vain,
> for God did not endow her with wisdom
>   or give her a share of good sense.
> Yet when she spreads her feathers to run,
>   she laughs at horse and rider."
>   (39:13–18)

"I did not make the ostrich with the best motherly instincts," says the Lord. "It was I who did not give the ostrich best wisdom and common sense, but I am the same Lord who made the ostrich able to run away from a horse and rider and laugh doing so. Please explain, Job." The servant Job is further amazed.

We have imagined in our Bible group how the face of the servant of God must have looked stunned when facing the fact that he was so inept to answer the queries of God. I am not able to adequately explain how we laughed, trying to imagine how much of a fool Job must have felt when put in his place. A "crisis" caused by God's revelation begins to dawn on Job. Some of my readers need to see the Lord and not just listen to or hear about God's Word.

The Lord said to Job:

> *"Will the one who contends with the Almighty*
> *correct him?*
> *Let him who accuses God answer him!"*

Then Job answered the Lord:

> *"I am unworthy—how can I reply to you?*
> *I put my hand over my mouth.*
> *I spoke once, but I have no answer—*
> *twice, but I will say no more."*
> (40:1–5)

The awesome power of God is on display in interacting with the man Job. God continues:

> *"Would you discredit my justice?*
> *Would you condemn me to justify yourself?*

Do you have an arm like God's,
  and can your voice thunder like his?
Then adorn yourself with glory and splendor,
  and clothe yourself in honor and majesty.
Unleash the fury of your wrath,
  look at all who are proud and bring them low,
look at all who are proud and humble them,
  crush the wicked where they stand.
Bury them all in the dust together;
  shroud their faces in the grave.
Then I myself will admit to you
  that your own right hand can save you."
  (40:8–14)

Again, Job is put on the ground by what is more prominent than him. Job is floored in the presentation.

One of my favorite chapters in the book of Job is chapter forty-one. I am fascinated by God's conversation with Job about the excellent sea animal called Leviathan. The animal is mentioned six times in the Bible (in the books of Job, Amos, Psalms, and Isaiah). As to the historical truths that surround the mystery of this ancient animal, I will leave to those scholars who spend time searching to understand better. I am fascinated by the immensity, power, and beauty of this animal that perhaps is like today's white whale.

"Can you pull in Leviathan with a fishhook

or tie down its tongue with a rope?
Can you put a cord through its nose
or pierce its jaw with a hook?
Will it keep begging you for mercy?
Will it speak to you with gentle words?
Will it make an agreement with you
for you to take it as your slave for life?
Can you make a pet of it like a bird
or put it on a leash for the young women in
your house?
Will traders barter for it?
Will they divide it up among the merchants?
Can you fill its hide with harpoons
or its head with fishing spears?
If you lay a hand on it,
you will remember the struggle and never
do it again!
Any hope of subduing it is false;
the mere sight of it is overpowering.
No one is fierce enough to rouse it.
Who then is able to stand against me?"
(41:1–10)

1. How vast are the creative facets of God, earth, sea, and sky, all in the parameters of His control!

2. How truly detailed is the creation of God! Nothing in detail is missed by Him.

3. God created His massive handiwork with so many parts. He did not go to sleep or watch from afar. He did not wind up the world as a toy and leave it to function on its own. God is in every detail of His creation and is responding all the time as He sees fit as the Sovereign of all.

4. The parts of Leviathan mentioned show the power involved in what God created and yet still shows how detailed-orientated is the care of God in providing the perfect playpen for this animal in the vast oceans. Listen to God describing Leviathan:

"I will not fail to speak of Leviathan's limbs,
its strength and its graceful form.
Who can strip off its outer coat?
Who can penetrate its double coat of armor?
Who dares open the doors of its mouth,
ringed about with fearsome teeth?
Its back has rows of shields
tightly sealed together; each is so close to the next
that no air can pass between.
They are joined fast to one another;
they cling together and cannot be parted.
Its snorting throws out flashes of light;
its eyes are like the rays of dawn.
Flames stream from its mouth;
sparks of fire shoot out.

Smoke pours from its nostrils
as from a boiling pot over burning reeds.
Its breath sets coals ablaze,
and flames dart from its mouth.
Strength resides in its neck;
dismay goes before it."
(41:12–22)

God does all the things that He has pointed out and more to Job. Is there anything outside God's purview? Can the eyes of God be covered from His perfect vision and the care of His children shortened? Jesus in the New Testament indicated that even the hairs on peoples' heads are correctly numbered. "Job, you see that I have not gone to sleep or abandoned you even in these days when you have been suffering and facing challenges beyond your comprehension." No one or anything will contain God.

The messages to the servant Job proclaim the truth of safely resting in the hands of God. He sees that he is perfectly safe in God's care. I am convinced that this was the place and time that the physical, emotional, and psychological healing for Job by God started, although not explicitly stated. A great crossroads had come in the growth of the life of Job. This season was a significant development for the remainder of his journey to grow deeper in his relationship with God.

Job was being shown a marvelous truth and principle. As I watched a beautiful and unusually colored bird in my backyard, feeding on what was on the ground, it steadily looked around, ensuring that there was no one or anything nearby that could be a danger. I was in a place where the bird could not see me, and it dawned on me that as much as the bird was caring for itself using its prowess, God was best caring for this creature, which could be outsmarted by circumstances bigger and smarter than itself. Correspondingly, we as human beings are alone in God's hands for complete safety—no matter how hard we try to "outsmart" life.

The spiritually hungry Job was being pushed to grow spiritually by using the illustrations of how God perfectly cares for His impressive and majestic creation. His daily unfailing intervention in His handiwork is one of the clear testimonies of how faithful our God is. In Job 40:14 God indicates to Job that his right hand cannot save him. That means that as excellent the characteristics of Job's life are (integrity, blamelessness, and righteousness), they are not what keeps securely, guards, and rewards this man's life. It is God's right hand alone that supplies and holds him through thick and thin. It is God's right hand that enables the servant Job to have a determined shameless audacity in the pitfalls and challenges offered in life. We see a beautiful picture or one foretaste of how inadequate we are without the power of the cross, which would be "God's perfect right hand" for the needs of the whole world. Hallelujah!

Truly, there is a profound mystery and joy in sharing in the suffering of our Lord Jesus Christ as His disciples. The apostle Paul writes, "Now I rejoice in my sufferings for you, and I am completing in my flesh what is lacking in Christ's afflictions for his body, that is, the church." (Colossians 1:24 CSB). Also, reflect on these verses:

> *God is our refuge and strength,*
> *an ever-present help in trouble.*
> *Therefore we will not fear, though*
> *the earth give way*
> *and the mountains fall into the heart of the sea.*
> (Psalm 46:1–2)

6

The Light that Engulfs Job
(Chapter 42)

Without chapter 42 the message in the truths from the book of Job would be incomplete. What do we see enclosed in this highly significant chapter? In the following passage are seen some very important truths to receiving light from the adventure and pitfalls that surrounded Job's life. Let that same light engulf you within the realities of your life. The light from God is intended not only for our conscious beings but also the unconscious parts of our lives that are higher than the tallest mountain and more profound than the deepest sea.

Then Job replied to the Lord:

> *"I know that you can do all things;*
> *no purpose of yours can be thwarted.*
> *You asked, 'Who is this that obscures my plans*
> *without knowledge?'*
> *Surely I spoke of things I did not understand,*
> *things too wonderful for me to know.*
>
> *You said, 'Listen now, and I will speak;*

I will question you,
*   and you shall answer me.'*
My ears had heard of you
*   but now my eyes have seen you.*
Therefore I despise myself
*   and repent in dust and ashes."* . . .

After Job had prayed for his friends, the Lord re-
stored his fortunes and gave him twice as much as
he had before. . . .

After this, Job lived a hundred and forty years; he
saw his children and their children to the fourth
generation. And so Job died, an old man and full
of years. (42: 1–6, 10, 16)

Let's imagine that the book of Job had closed different-
ly. Suppose verses 7–17 had merely said that Job died after
his confession and confrontation by God. Everything else
in the text remained the same. Would it have mattered hundreds of years later how the end of Job came about? I will let
you decide.

In noting the profound revelations given in the Holy
Writ, I hope there is a keen appreciation that behind all suffering, catastrophes, pain, sicknesses, and injustices is the allowing hand of God. The providential care of God means that
nothing awful and painful in our lives gets outside the sight

of God and that He allows all things to happen—and if He does not, then they will not happen.

Some things that God allows are bad from a human perspective and intended by outside evil forces for our evil, but nothing is outside God's perfect providence, even when human eyes cannot see or understand. As I write this paragraph, I testify to appreciating that I may not have far to go in my earthly journey, but my eternal hope gets sweeter in my expectancy to see and be with Jesus. Only God determines those details in the lives of individuals. That knowledge gives peace to my soul.

Psalm 116:10 says, "I trusted in the Lord when I said, I am greatly afflicted." I read this verse as a part of my devotional time in *Our Daily Bread*, written by Amy Peterson (October 10, 2018, devotional). She tells this story:

> *Two men convicted of drug trafficking had been on death row for a decade. While in prison, they learned of God's love for them in Jesus, and their lives were transformed. When it came time for them to face the firing squad, they faced their executioners reciting the Lord's Prayer and singing "Amazing Grace." Because of their faith in God, through the power of the Spirit, they were able to face death with incredible courage.*

God decides the time for facing death for all of us, and my prayer is that we will have incredible inner courage when our hour comes. With boldness, may God's children today have a shameless audacity in loving God in the pitfalls and challenges of this life. May that daring courage take us through the door of death as we hold on tightly to the hands of Jesus and as He holds us tightly.

For those who have been mistreated in this life, remember wholeheartedly another hard-to-understand but pointed message. Jesus shares this parable in Luke 18:1–8:

> *"In a certain town there was a judge who neither feared God nor cared what people thought. And there was a widow in that town who kept coming to him with the plea, 'Grant me justice against my adversary.' For some time he refused. But finally he said to himself, 'Even though I don't fear God or care what people think, yet because this widow keeps bothering me, I will see that she gets justice, so that she won't eventually come and attack me!'"* And the Lord said, *"Listen to what the unjust judge says. And will not God bring about justice for his chosen ones, who cry out to him day and night? Will he keep putting them off? I tell you, he will see that they get justice, and quickly. However, when the Son of Man comes, will he find faith on the earth?"*

The parable above is mentioned because there are those who are still baffled by the unfairness of life, even from within the body of Christ. Let's remember that it is not that God is taking your queries lightly but that there are sometimes much more significant issues in the eternal scheme of things than what you are now facing. Therefore, stand firm in your faith in God with your shameless audacity of loving God as you go through difficult days. Do not ever think that our good heavenly Father would give His child a snake when he or she has asked Him so long for a fish. (Remember Luke 11:11–13.)

Like the all-knowing God, this makes the actions of God perfect and without fault, as acknowledged by Job (42:3). Not even the saintly Job in his intimate relationship with God could thwart the will of God, and it is this truth that he accepted being a willing and abandoned servant or love slave of the heavenly Master. Job in that same verse indicates that he had spoken from years of spiritual, emotional, and physical maturity, but he had been stopped in his boots by the light of God's questioning in chapters 38–41.

The servant Job came to appreciate how inadequate his assumptions had been and how far ahead God was in handling everything, even in the great injustices of life. As such, Job stopped speaking and repented in thinking that he knew so much. His soul had ventured into believing that he could "trace God" or try to follow God but was indeed not able to keep up. We reflect similarly on King David in Psalm 51. Job was full of remorse, which led him to marvel at God's grace and not remain in a state of self-defeat. Both Job and David had victory in repenting thoroughly before God. Job showed his brokenness in 42:6.

A real jewel to treasure is this statement by C. S. Lewis: "The true Christian's nostril is to be continually attentive to the inner cesspool." I know Job did not like the smell of sin and all that is involved in willfully falling short, but it is a necessary smell we need to be aware of for any serious Christian. A cesspit for each of us includes anything that rivals the will of God in our lives.

Job willingly yielded to the divine map for his life, a diagram instituted by God's plan for him after he was shown the more profound facts that count. Our self-surrender each day to the lordship of Christ in our lives is a choice each of us must make. Sometimes challenges and pitfalls come, and a Whisper asks us, "Do you still trust Me with all you have surrendered?"

A surrendered life to Christ is a delivered life. A submitted life to Christ is one devoted to God regardless of what happens. An abandoned life to Christ is one determined that even in death, "I am still moving forward knowing that I am cared for by my God."

The Word says in Colossians 2:6–10,

> So then, just as you received Christ Jesus as
> Lord, continue to live your lives in him, rooted and

built up in him, strengthened in the faith as you were taught, and overflowing with thankfulness. See to it that no one takes you captive through hollow and deceptive philosophy, which depends on human tradition and the elemental spiritual forces of this world rather than on Christ. For in Christ all the fullness of the Deity lives in bodily form, and in Christ you have been brought to fullness [which works perfectly when a believer faces pitfalls].

"Spiritual truth is learned through the atmosphere that surrounds us, not through intellectual reasoning. It is God's Spirit that changes the atmosphere of our way of looking at things, and then things begin to be possible which before were impossible" (Oswald Chambers, *My Utmost for His Highest*, October 12 devotional).

Be reminded again of John 11, which records how Jesus dealt with the death and resurrection of Lazarus and the great pain He faced seeing the family and friends suffer in their tragic loss. Jesus was silent for days, and the family did not know the great miracle that was going to happen before their eyes. Moved by the emotions in the home and community, Jesus began to cry (John 11:35).

I wonder if God the Father also cried having to see Job suffer so much and not able to tell earlier a more important story that would bring greater glory to Him. I wonder about

Jesus crying for many of His servants facing hell-like pitfalls and circumstances in which He was not able to reveal at the time all that was going on. That is why I am satisfied knowing that the New Testament teaches us that while we see life darkly or incompletely, one day we will better understand: "For now we see only a reflection as in a mirror; then we shall see face to face. Now I know in part; then I shall know fully, even as I am fully known" (1 Corinthians 13:12).

Job knew for many of his mature years that he had lived a very blessed life and had seen so much of God's favor and had now reached a stubborn and "hard rock" season in his life. God had awakened him as to how far he had gone from appreciating his worth by God and that he was still the center of God's joy. Although Job had not committed sin, he was broken, repentant, and sorrowful for losing a great sense of what he should not have. I can imagine Job asking God to take him back to where he first believed and to the first place merely being in love with God.

It is a beautiful personal experience brought to the place of humility before God and His grace. Repentance or contrition is a part of the gifts and beauty of God. For Christians who do not know how to exhibit thorough remorse in their Christian journey, I lovingly encourage going back to Calvary. Pray for "the gift of tears" that in earlier seasons was prayed for by the Puritans. There is no holiness without knowing how to repent at specific points of life walking hand in hand with Jesus. Remember the old song that says, "We need to hear from You."

"Listen to advice and accept discipline, and at the end you will be counted among the wise. Many are the plans in a person's heart, but it is the Lord's purpose that prevails" (Proverbs 19:20–21). Paul states from another vantage point, "I want to know Christ—yes, to know the power of his resurrection and participation in his sufferings, becoming like him in his death, and so, somehow, attaining to the resurrection from the dead" (Philippians 3:10–11).

The place to receiving the best from this book of Job is found in the words of Job: "My ears had heard of you, but now my eyes have seen you (42:5). This grand vision received by Job led to a repentant heart and subsequent growth by the servant of God. We must zero in on the massive difference between hearing about the truths of God and seeing or perceiving God in the midst of what He is trying to teach us for a better heart and lifestyle. Job saw that it is God behind everything going on, and God had not forgotten him in his adversity.

I have no idea what the scenario was when God spoke directly to Job. However, it happened, and Job knew that it was not an angel speaking or some other holy person, but God Himself, and he was in the presence of the holiness of the Holy. As I attempt to comment on the actual situation, which is way bigger than me, the best way to reflect is to look at what happened when other persons saw God. You can also see God in a personal and new direction.

Isaiah 6:1–5 says,

> *In the year that King Uzziah died, I saw the Lord, high and exalted, seated on a throne; and the train of his robe filled the temple. Above him were seraphim, each with six wings: With two wings they covered their faces, with two they covered their feet, and with two they were flying. And they were calling to one another:*
>
> *"Holy, holy, holy is the Lord Almighty; the whole earth is full of his glory."*
>
> *At the sound of their voices the doorposts and thresholds shook and the temple was filled with smoke.*
>
> *"Woe to me!" I cried. "I am ruined! For I am a man of unclean lips, and I live among a people of unclean lips, and my eyes have seen the King, the Lord Almighty."*

Out of this awesome encounter that Isaiah perceived, the heart and mouth of the prophet Isaiah were cleansed, and he willingly responded to the call of God to share the Word of God with the people of God no matter what the cost was.

Psalm 63:2–5 says, "I have seen you in the sanctuary and beheld your power and your glory. Because your love is better than life, my lips will glorify you. I will praise you as long as I live, and in your name, I will lift up my hands. I will be fully satisfied as with the richest of foods with singing lips my mouth will praise you."

Out of this remarkable encounter the heart and mouth of King David perceived and testified to his satisfaction and gratitude with God above everything else in this life and that he loved God more than his own life.

Genesis 32:30 says, "Jacob called the place Peniel, saying, 'It is because I saw God face to face, and yet my life was spared.'"

Out of this sublime encounter the heart and the mouth of Jacob perceived and were never the same. He suffered from a limp for the rest of his life, and he knew the pain inflicted was to help bring glory to the world in a fresh new way for God's purpose.

John 20:19–22 says,

> *On the evening of that first day of the week, when the disciples were together, with the doors locked for fear of the Jewish leaders, Jesus came and stood among them and said, "Peace be with you!" After he said this, he showed them his hands and side. The disciples were thrilled when they saw the Lord. Again Jesus said, "Peace be with you!*

*As the Father has sent me, I am sending you." And
with that, he breathed on them and said, "Receive
the Holy Spirit."*

In this remarkable encounter our resurrected Lord and
God appeared to some of His closest disciples, and this
brought joy beyond words when they saw the Lord. This passage was one of the post-resurrection appearances that empowered the disciples to wait in Jerusalem until all were filled
with the Holy Spirit in the Upper Room. Out of this experience Jesus's glorious church was born and is still carrying on
His mission even within the pitfalls and challenges of life.

As Jesus saw during our journey and its struggles, we are
invigorated with new power and enthusiasm and courage in
a trip that has dark days. Our encouragement is to live a broken, humble, daring, courageous, and Spirit-filled life in the
pitfalls and challenges of life. Have you seen or perceived that
truth in your life?

The apostle John wrote the words of Jesus: "In the world
you will have tribulation, but take courage; I have overcome
the world" (John 16:33 NASB). The book of Job has been
telling us that joyful Christian living is not always deliverance
from all adversity.

Facing adversity is true to the faith journey. A holy life
as seen in the example of Job is living victoriously amid difficulty and the hard days we all must face. Each reader should

allow each part of our journey to become a protected secret place inhabited by the power of God. Someone put it well: "If there is no strain, there is no strength." Job grasped the depth of this truth. He grew to appreciate further that faith never knows where it's to be led but loves the shameless audacity exhibited in loving the One who is driving. Take hold of the undisciplined nature in your soul and grow as Jesus guides your daily life.

Do you also fully appreciate like Job that God can withdraw His physical blessings from us and our trust in Christ is not negatively affected? Make that personal commitment now to love God even if you lose everything else. Renew that commitment today if you have not done so already. Are you willing to pay the price for full consecration to God and His sanctification of your life? As with Job's example, will the nature and character of Jesus overshadow and control you?

In bringing this Bible book to its end, the text reads,

> *After the Lord had said these things to Job, he said to Eliphaz the Temanite, "I am angry with you and your two friends because you have not spoken the truth about me, as my servant Job has. So now take seven bulls and seven rams and go to my servant Job and sacrifice a burnt offering for yourselves. My servant Job will pray for you, and I will accept his prayer and not deal with you according to your folly. You have not spoken the truth about me, as*

my servant Job has." So Eliphaz the Temanite, Bildad the Shuhite and Zophar the Naamathite did what the Lord told them; and the Lord accepted Job's prayer. After Job had prayed for his friends, the Lord restored his fortunes and gave him twice as much as he had before. (42:7–10)

A few points for our sober reflection:

1. "Therefore confess your sins to each other and pray for each other so that you may be healed. The prayer of a righteous person is powerful and effective" (James 5:16). Job is a wonderful example of the prayers of a righteous person. I love the words written by Millard Erickson on the matter of prayer: "In prayer, real prayer, we begin to think God's thoughts after him: to desire the things he desires, to love the things he loves, to will the things he wills." The will of God was done for the friends of Job. It was God who spoke directly to Eliphaz to go with his friends to seek the intercession of Job.

   The intercessory involvement of the patriarch is a testimony for children of God who trust and obey Him today. Please do not lose sight that God did not see the three friends of Job as "bad guys" who deserved punishment, but misguided and misinformed followers of God who needed to be given the privilege again of full nurturing by God's hands. Keep praying powerfully and continually today for others when you are at your weakest physically.

In the story of Job it is incredible to realize that Job's friends had been used by Satan for a period to further inflict suffering and heartfelt destruction by their innuendos and misleading accusations. Again, remember to be aware that sometimes lousy advice can come from well-intentioned Christian people. Have a loving and forgiving heart if this happens to you. Many years ago my oldest daughter, Stephanie, brought home from school a statement written by Napoleon Hill that says, "If you must speak ill of another, do not speak it . . . write it in the sand near the water's edge." I have never forgotten it.

2. In today's United States a quote by Henri Nouwen helps to remind us that we live in many communities that unfortunately say loud and clear, "You are no good; you are ugly in one way or another; you are worthless; you are despicable; you are nobody—unless you demonstrate the opposite." The writer of this quote wants us to be honest with ourselves.

The attitude of Job was the opposite of the previous quote regarding what our country is presently saying in diverse ways. Job delighted in God and was such a blessing to his generation and every culture and time that have followed. Are we listening and noting that we must speak more lovingly in our reaching out of hands to others who are different?

With all the brokenness, failures, and sins of our own past lives, can God make our lives courageous in our love for our Savior? Yes, the grace of God frees us from the past failures in our walk with God and helps us to fiercely and audaciously love and serve God today.

3. After the ministry of intercession by Job, the Lord restored his fortunes and gave him twice as much as he had before. It is also clear that God healed him of all his physical ailments. Praise the Lord! Job got to live a further one hundred forty years and saw the beauty of his heritage after his terrible experiences. For the dangerous situations and background that engulfed Job, one has to shout with joy that God was kind enough to fully heal and restore Job to more than he had before

Unfortunately, stories of the snags and drawbacks of other people's lives do not have the same ending. In today's world there are not many joyful and happy older people unless they know Jesus as their Lord and Savior. How the journey ends is done well only in the control of the hands of God. How the journey continues perfectly into eternity is beautiful beyond the comprehension of anyone as it was for Job and all faithful disciples of Christ.

There are so many of Jesus's parables that are rich, pointed, and powerful. The following is another that every reader who identifies in one form or another with the life and example of the patriarch Job should reread many times. Jesus said,

"The kingdom of heaven is like a landowner who went out early in the morning to hire workers for his vineyard. He agreed to pay them a denarius for the day and sent them into his vineyard. About nine in the morning he went out and saw others standing in the marketplace doing nothing. He told them, 'You also go and work in my vineyard, and I will pay you whatever is right.' So they went. He went out again about noon and about three in the afternoon and did the same thing. About five in the afternoon he went out and found still others standing around. He asked them, 'Why have you been standing here all day long doing nothing?'

"'Because no one has hired us,' they answered.

"He said to them, 'You also go and work in my vineyard.'

"When evening came, the owner of the vineyard said to his foreman, 'Call the workers and pay them their wages, beginning with the last ones hired and going on to the first.'

"The workers who were hired about five in the

afternoon came, and each received a denarius. So when those came who were hired first, they expected to receive more. But each one of them also received a denarius. When they received it, they began to grumble against the landowner. 'These who were hired last worked only one hour,' they said, 'and you have made them equal to us who have borne the burden of the work and the heat of the day.'

"But he answered one of them, 'I am not being unfair to you, friend. Didn't you agree to work for a denarius? Take your pay and go. I want to give the one who was hired last the same as I gave you. Don't I have the right to do what I want with my own money? Or are you envious because I am generous?'

"So the last will be first, and the first will be last."

(Matthew 20:1–16)

The old song says, "It's a high way to heaven . . . None can walk up there but the pure in hearts." Shameless audacity in our love for Jesus helps to keep our hearts pure. Everything will see a culmination designed by God; therefore, let us live holy and godly lives in all the details of our existence. Yes, outward disturbances and roadblocks are a part of your journey. Therefore, live by faith in Jesus and practice shameless audacity, and there will be no struggles that will overcome your soul.

If there were never any clouds in our lives, we would have no faith. "His way is in the whirlwind and the storm, and clouds are the dust of his feet" (Nahum 1:3). They are a sign that God is there. What a revelation it is to know that sorrow, bereavement, and suffering are actually the clouds that come along with God! God cannot come near us without clouds [shadows]—He does not come in clear-shining brightness.

(Oswald Chambers, *My Utmost for His Highest*, July 29 devotional)

A disciple of Christ doesn't know the joy of the Lord in spite of tribulation but because of it. Paul said, "I am exceedingly joyful in all our tribulation" (2 Corinthians 7:4 NKJV).

7

The Loud Message to the Blessed One
(Psalm 1)

As we have journeyed with Job, we have been exposed to the truth from the heart of God in the Scriptures and challenged. How do you take the light afforded through the life of Job and make it personal to your present faith-walk for the rest of your days?

Living through suffering, pitfalls, and challenges is not easy, and it goes with being a human being. Sometimes the traps and falls are more profound for others than we can appreciate, but the same God who was there for Job is the same God who wants to walk victoriously with each of us. Even when someone hates and is vile to you in your journey, there is a victory through the merits of the cross. I am merely saying that we should expect delays and detours in our trip through life as one of Christ's disciples. When those pitfalls come, you are being challenged to be bold in your confidence and trust in our Lord and Savior.

Jesus loves us in the present tense, but often we are prone to forget and sometimes drift unless we have a stable anchor like the messages and principles shown in the book of Job. Every day we need to look inwardly at our love for Jesus. Abide in Jesus's love for your security. The faith we are challenged to copy as seen in Job is way beyond an intellectual idea. With the help of the Holy Spirit, the guidance from Job is solid ground to bolster our deepest convictions and holy lifestyle even in the pitfalls of life.

> *For every detail of common sense in life, there is a truth God has revealed by which we can prove in our practical experience what we believe God to be. Faith is a tremendously active principle that always puts Jesus Christ first. The life of faith says, "Lord, You have said it, it appears to be irrational, but I'm going to step out boldly, trusting in Your Word" (for example, see Matthew 6:33). Turning intellectual faith into our possession is always a fight, not just sometimes.* (Oswald Chambers, *My Utmost for His Highest*, October 30 devotional)

There are some things each of us must be willing to do. At this intersection the shameless audacity of our love for Jesus needs to be a clear choice that each of us must make without reservation.

After journeying in the Scriptures, I am convinced that it is not by accident that Psalm 1 follows the book of Job. Psalm 1 starts with the words "Blessed is the one . . ." To live as a blessed person is a lifestyle when all is said and done, which will give you the greatest happiness and joy and will be a solid rock in the days of your journey.

The servant Job is someone blessed, and you are challenged to be another person who is blessed by God. In this conversation the word *blessed* means having the favor of God. One of the best ways for appreciating the Beatitudes (a part of Matthew 5–7) is Jesus speaking on the mount to the people gathered, saying in different ways that those "having the favor of God" are those who live the way He is instructing. "Live the way Job lived" is what the apostle James would also bluntly and fearlessly tell us.

Let our focus now be on the words of Psalm 1:

> *Blessed is the one*
> *who does not walk in step with the wicked*
> *or stand in the way that sinners take*
> *or sit in the company of mockers,*
> *but whose delight is in the law of the Lord,*
> *and who meditates on his law day and night.*
> *That person is like a tree planted by streams of*
> *water,*
> *which yields its fruit in season*
> *and whose leaf does not wither—*
> *whatever they do prospers.*
>
> *Not so the wicked!*

They are like chaff
that the wind blows away.
Therefore the wicked will not stand in the
judgment,
nor sinners in the assembly of the righteous.

For the Lord watches over the way of the righteous,
but the way of the wicked leads to destruction.
(Psalm 1:1–6)

Anyone who absorbs Psalm 1 understands that the blessed one is the person who walks away and stands far from a sinful lifestyle and does not sit with or fellowship continuously with ungodly people.

The blessed one delights in the Word of God every single day. The fortunate person will not stay away from the directions of the Holy Bible. Each day the Word of God is the central direction for the life of the blessed one. The Word of God nourishes the outer life and inner person each day. A holy person will read the Bible not for a "happy and intellectual ride" but for the sustaining of his or her life.

The blessed person lives each moment in the power and presence of the Holy Spirit. The blessed one is empowered and guided by all the Holy Spirit instructs. The Holy Spirit is God Almighty who yearns and will sanctify wholly each man and woman who will commit his or her will and body to all that God requires. The Holy Spirit will purge thoroughly every sin the person is born with and all uncontrollable sin in a believer's life as all is surrendered to Him.

With the presence and power of the Holy Spirit filling the person, he or she will exhibit the life of our Lord Jesus Christ boldly in his or her body. In 1 Corinthians 9:27 we read, "I discipline my body and bring it into subjection" (NKJV). The whole of our being is the actual temple of the Holy Spirit (1 Corinthians 6:19), and this includes our desires, thoughts, and actions even when our physical bodies become weak and frail. In your struggles allow the Holy Spirit to help you judge yourself harder at all times than you judge others, even those who have hurt you a lot in life.

The heavenly fragrance and favor of God do not go away from anyone who lives trusting and obeying as His blessed child. The personality at the core of your being and your normal behavior lives abundantly in God's favor as a holy person.

On the other hand, the man or woman who is not a blessed one does not have any of the Spirit-filled protection and support mentioned. A narcissistic person is not a holy person in God's eyes, but Jesus invites that person to deliverance from sin, plus redemption and satisfaction at the cross.

Hallelujah to God for even the detours of our lives, which have been given by God to the blessed man or woman who lives among us today. If you have suffered long, there is no one stopping you from being a blessed one, except yourself. It is now time for you to solidify your life as shameless and audacious in your love for and faith in Jesus Christ.

What have we seen from the life of Job in the book named after him?

1. God loved the servant Job so much and delighted in him continuously.

2. The devil hated Job very much, and he will curse you too as you intimately walk with Christ.

3. The Lord had daily fellowship with Job, and love showed both ways.

4. The blessed Job faced great adversity for a profound season. Trouble is something everyone must meet at some point in various seasons.

5. In Job's days there were sinful and wicked people also. Interestingly, even in Job's worst days his closest communications were with God's people.

6. Godly friends can sometimes make mistakes in the counsel they give. Be careful and wise in giving and receiving counsel, blessed one.

7. The blessed Job went through bitter suffering. This fact often goes hand in hand with the lives of God's children in the twenty-first century.

8. Walking in God's light and the bitterness of suffering you face will not overcome you.

What must we receive internally from the example of Job?

1. The servant Job was a blessed man in the midst of having plenty and in the days when he did not know when would be his last breath.

2. Humility was a cornerstone to the life of Job being a blessed one.

3. The humble Job came to appreciate the sovereignty and providential care of God in a refreshed and profound way. Nothing is too intense for God or beyond His complete attention.

4. We have observed that a constant willingness to genuinely repent before God is a hallmark of a blessed person.

5. The willingness to be a real blessing to other people is a hallmark of a blessed person.

6. A blessed person stands in the will of God daily and allows Christ to favor you with what He sees as best for you.

7. No matter how high the storms and waves are raging in your life, allow God to give you peace, as He did His servant Job.

8. Remember always that "By my God I can leap over every wall" (Psalm 18:29, author's paraphrase).

We have been reading about God's blessed revelation through sharing with the life of Job. God intended for us to receive blessed hope for our entire journey in this life. John Wesley (a great historical preacher, teacher, and missionary for Christ who has had a tremendous effect on my theological background) once said very well, "The world hopes for the best, but the Lord offers the best hope." Hallelujah! In the faithfulness of God put your hope.

Go through everything and every day trusting in Jesus with eternal love. It is your time for Jesus, more of Jesus, and more intimacy with Jesus through life for the remainder of your days. In your life before others and when no one is looking, declare your authenticity and shameless audacity of faith in Jesus.

For all of God's disciples in your worst days and deepest pitfalls, remember that God does not fail in fulfilling the vision and insights He has given you. Oswald Chambers puts it well:

> *God gives us a vision, and then He takes us down to the valley to batter us into the shape of that vision. It is in the valley that so many of us give up and faint. Every God-given vision will become real if we will only have patience. Just think of the enormous amount of free time God has! He is never in a hurry. Yet we are always in such a frantic hurry.*

While still in the light of the glory of the vision, we go right out to do things, but the vision is not yet real in us. God has to take us into the valley and put us through fires and floods to batter us into shape, until we get to the point where He can trust us with the reality of the vision. Ever since God gave us the vision, He has been at work. He is getting us into the shape of the goal He has for us, and yet over and over again we try to escape from the Sculptor's hand to batter ourselves into the shape of our own goal.

The vision that God gives is not some unattainable castle in the sky, but a vision of what God wants you to be down here. Allow the Potter to put you on His wheel and whirl you around as He desires. Then as surely as God is God, and you are you, you will turn out as an exact likeness of the vision. But don't lose heart in the process. If you have ever had a vision from God, you may try as you will to be satisfied on a lower level, but God will never allow it. (Oswald Chambers, *My Utmost for His Highest*, July 6 devotional)

Be shameless and audacious in allowing and fulfilling the vision and view for this life He has promised to you. As with Job, your pitfall may seem only to be parched ground now, but remember that even those tough grounds will become a pool and oasis and a place of growth in God's divine hand. (Isaiah 35:7)

8

Life Testimonies

God's revelation from the book of Job changes and refreshes the lives of people who read with a pang of hunger to obey God's will. Please write down your testimony after soaking your soul in the Word from the book of Job. I would love to receive your testimony to be encouraged in my spiritual journey. Please send yours to me at *sluggymorgan@aol.com*.

The following declaration is from the heart of **Mrs. Ann Morgan**:

> *For me, the book of Job for a long time was merely an account of his losses in chapters 1 and 2 and the restoration of his blessings in chapter 42. The middle sections were just words. It was only one of the books you go through as you are reading through the Bible each year. Having gone through an in-depth study of Job, I find that the middle chapters now have so much more meaning.*
>
> *I am so grateful that we took the time to "break it down and chew it up." There is so much in this*

book that is timeless and shows the condition of the human heart today. Here are some things which stood out to me as we studied:

God's people can give bad advice. We often think of Job's friends as accusers, but they were godly people, only misguided by what they saw, and passed judgment on Job without knowing the facts. Have you been there? Have you been falsely judged and demeaned by "good people" who didn't know what they are talking about? Let's be careful with how we treat each other in the family of God. We should pour in the "oil and wine" on the wounded, not "sulfur and vinegar."

The man Job was suffering physical, emotional, and mental pain from not understanding the "why" behind the suffering, and then he had to face emotional pain from the accusations of his friends. The example of the life of Job has been such a growing point for me. Lord, let me never again stand in the shoes of Job's friends but learn to be compassionate to those who appear to be on the wrong side of the track.

No matter how difficult the circumstance, once you are walking with God, nothing can happen to you unless God allows it. Job received galvanization in his faith. In the face of the accusations, he would not flinch. "Though he slay me, yet will I trust in him" (Job 13:15 KJV). Job trusted in God altogether.

I am asking my Lord to give me Job-like faith that will not falter.

The following testimony is from the heart of **Mr. Anthony Turrentine**:

The book of Job has inspired me to follow the life example of the patriarch Job, no matter the cost. Now in my sixties, I am at the stage in my life journey that no matter how much I am given or do not have, I am going to stay close to Jesus. I will belong to Jesus through my suffering, trials, and any loss or gains that God allows.

I know that I will not be as righteous as Job throughout his life, but when I accepted Jesus as my Savior He freed me from all my sins and made me honest through His blood shed for me on the cross. Job's experience has shown me the importance of enduring the many challenging things that will come my way. That will include family problems, financial burdens, and health issues. As Job found comfort in the Lord, I am determined to stay confident trusting in Jesus for every situation and in every area each day for the rest of my life.

I have worked two jobs for the past twenty years and have been away from home most of the time; I've learned to put my trust in God, who provides shelter and direction as I come and go. The time away from family can be very stressful and lonely, and the care of my family and me is in God's hands. To work in New York and live in Pennsylvania is not easy.

God is giving me a Job-like spirit knowing that I leave my journey in His hands and give my talents and spiritual gifts to be used as God sees best. My Savior is teaching me more and more patience, perseverance, and endurance.

There have been many days that I feel like I cannot go on. Sometimes I feel like throwing in the towel facing pain and sleepless nights. But Job has been a great help in drawing me closer to God and allowing His wonder-working power seen from my innermost being.

My prayer is that God's favor toward me will continue to increase as I worship in deed and word. He has continued to keep me from falling asleep as I shared with my Bible study group and almost died.

Living life so busily has not stopped me from making myself ready to help others as God prompts.

He has given me so much mercy, grace, and love, and I pray to keep open to help other people just as Job did in the Bible.

I have been encouraged so much in my spiritual walk during my study of the book of Job. I pray the same for all others as you study thoroughly the Word of God.

The following is the testimony from the heart of **Mr. Durwin Edwards**:

This book describes the spiritual warfare Job went through at a deep level. The author highlights well the journey of Job through interpreting the scripture, poems, songs of praise, offering of prayer, and so on. Going through the book of Job has promoted a sharper focus for readers like me. I have grown to appreciate a better understanding of Job's testings and his fellowship with God, but above all, Job's determined resolution to be accurate to his Lord and Master.

With all honesty I lost so much along the journey of my life. I admit being deceived by faulty counseling and the challenges brought through financial hardship and some health afflictions.

Years ago I had brain surgery, went into a coma, and became paralyzed from my neck down. There have been so much back pain, painful swellings, and other hurts from numerous illnesses. If you saw me now, you would not believe how God has helped me to walk and process my daily tasks. I do have severe scars as a reminder as to how far I have come. God gave me a second chance.

But in my journey at one point I lost hope; I was distracted and many times upset and put down. Even in reflecting on the many miracles the Lord blessed me with, I forgot my spiritual footing, and there were times when I fell into depression with a broken heart.

Rudy's book provides biblical references to focus on. It has been light for my journey and a reflection and reminder of how deep and vast is God's love for me and other children of Christ. God's faithfulness, justice, provisions, and promises are beyond comparison. In my times of trouble, I needed something like God's Word in this book to uplift my spirit and redirect my steps.

I had a hunger for solutions, and the Lord provided me with this book as a point of reference that I surely needed. I enjoyed this book so such as it speaks with passion from an author who has been a friend for a long time.

It is my prayer that all readers of this book develop a deeper understanding of the heart of God as He searches the hearts of readers and helps them to fulfill His purpose for them in the growth of God's kingdom.

Conclusion

In each reader's life it is important to remember to pray first each day and often every day. In every pitfall and challenge, remember that prayer is your most potent weapon against our common enemy, the devil. Please pray with me right now depending on the help of the Holy Spirit.

Our loving and gracious heavenly Father,

You alone are our Savior and Redeemer. In Your arms we find Your endless love and grace. Thank You every day for pouring out blessings seen and unseen. You are there closer than the very air we breathe. There has not been a day that You have not cared perfectly morning, noon, and night in each of our lives. Thank You for Your great mercies and faithfulness.

You know intimately every pitfall and challenge that is happening in my life. Thank You for the light we have received reading about the life of Your servant Job. Thank You for his example and great encouragement. We understand that as much as Job suffered, he did not hurt as much as our Lord Jesus did, which led to His death on the cross for our every sin. Through Jesus I have full redemption. Praise the Lord!

You understand where each of us is today in our shameless audacity in our love for You. Please break down every wall that would interfere with our complete submission to You and our total dependence on You and the Word of God.

Please give a fresh touch from heaven in each of our souls. We hunger and ask for a mighty contact from You that will cause our lives to be ablaze in bringing only glory to Jesus Christ in our daily lives. Help us find the courage to follow You and share Your love with those around us.

For those who are physically hurting and in great pain, would You grant a miracle from the very heart of heaven? Take away miraculously the hurts as You see best, but even with the hurts You do not heal, let me be filled with hope in my life today and in the tomorrows. Please help each person to see Jesus beyond each obstacle and pitfall. O Lord, help each man and woman who has read this book to will to be God's sacrifice or "poured out like a drink offering" (2 Timothy 4:6) *in shameless obedience.*

O Father, please enable that the noblest dreams of victory in Christ be born in my life each day as I walk through the fires and challenges in this life. Please help in a compelling way each of us to fully adhere to "Trust in the Lord with all your heart and lean not on your understanding; in all your ways submit to him, and he will make your paths straight. Do not be wise in your own eyes; fear the Lord and shun evil" (Proverbs 3:5–7).

O Lord, please continue to strengthen my life. Jesus, please help me to trust and obey You even when I don't understand.

In the mighty name of King Jesus, our Savior, I pray with great gratitude.

"We know that in all things God works for the good of those who love him, who have been called according to his purpose" (Romans 8:28).

Remember also with certainty what is ahead for all of God's children who with shameless audacity love God throughout the pitfalls and challenges of life.

"Then the angel showed me the river of the water of life, as clear as crystal, flowing from the throne of God and of the Lamb. . . . No longer will there be any curse [no more suffering and pitfalls]. . . . He who testifies to these things says, 'Yes, I am coming soon.' Amen. Come, Lord Jesus. The grace of the Lord Jesus be with God's people. Amen" (Revelation 22:1, 3, 20–21).

As a shameless and audacious servant of Christ, choose willingly to pursue godly righteousness and God's love so that you may have an abundant life now and in eternity (Proverbs 21:21).

Some years ago a person said to me, "I will live until I die, and when I die live." I have never forgotten that, and I hope you will remember it also. "Blessed is the one who perseveres under trial because, having stood the test, that person will receive the crown of life that the Lord has promised to those who love him" (James 1:12).

Jesus was, Jesus is, and Jesus is the One to come.
Live in Jesus's arms all your days.

ABOUT THE AUTHOR

Rudy Morgan was born to Dr. John and Mrs. Pearl Morgan in Jamaica, West Indies, in 1958. He has been a disciple of Christ since his conversion in 1972 and continued the faith journey due to the grace of God. He was called to preach and minister the gospel in 1975. Presently he is involved in the planting of a sixth Church of the Nazarene in Cambria Heights, Queens, New York.

He has been married to Ann since 1980, and they have two grown children they are very proud of: Stephanie, who is married to Jay; and Casey. His love for Jesus is paramount, and he continues to serve others in every way that God allows.

He has been an ordained elder in the Church of the Nazarene since 1984 and has an earned Ph.D. in biblical studies. He loves to preach and teach the Word of God.

Your feedback and questions are welcomed at *sluggymorgan@aol.com.*

Made in the USA
Middletown, DE
30 December 2019

82263261R00097